Employment Contracts

for The New World of Work

First published in 2021.

ISBN: 978-1-86922-899-6 (Printed)
eISBN: 978-1-86922-900-9 (PDF ebook)

Published by KR Publishing
P O Box 3954
Randburg
2125
Republic of South Africa

Tel: (011) 706-6009
Fax: (011) 706-1127
E-mail: orders@knowres.co.za
Website: www.kr.co.za

Typesetting, layout and design: Cia Joubert, cia@knowres.co.za
Cover design: Marlene De Lorme, marlene@knowres.co.za
Editing and Proofreading: Jennifer Renton, jenniferrenton@live.co.za
Project management: Cia Joubert, cia@knowres.co.za

Employment Contracts

for The New World of Work

by

Jan Kemp Nel (Snr) & Jan Kemp Nel (Jnr)

2021

TABLE OF CONTENTS

ABOUT THE AUTHORS

Jan Kemp Nel (Snr)

Jan Kemp Nel (Snr), BA, LLB (UP) and Dip LR (Unisa), has extensive experience of the dynamics and practices of employment and labour relations law, and is a specialist in contract of employment law, in which he has been specializing for over the last 35 years. During this time, he was involved in a multitude of both CCMA and Labour Court cases and skirmishes, trials and settlements representing employers, employees and trade unions alike. He has also developed and introduced strategies and systems designed for optimal quality in employment relations generally. He advocates and practices a preventative structured approach, recognizing that conflict is inherent but that conflicts can always be resolved. Jan is also the author of *The Dismissal: A Practical and Informative Toolkit to Ensure a Fair and Effective Dismissal*, and *Win at the CCMA: An Easy Step-by-Step Guide*, as well as a book on practical absenteeism strategies *Reduce Absenteeism*.

Jan Kemp Nel (Jnr)

Jan Kemp Nel (Jnr), is a passionate and energetic new generation Attorney. He is also a labour law specialist, and an Admitted Attorney of the High Court of South Africa. He holds an LL.M degree. In addition to his busy South African schedule, he consults internationally on comparative Contract, Sport and Commercial Law, bringing with him a wealth of experience and decision making skills.

CHAPTER 1

INTRODUCTION AND OVERVIEW

In this introductory chapter, the canvas is provided for the quintessential elements of the employment relationship, inclusive of a brief overview of the history and origins of the contract of service or employment, the *locatio conductio operarum,* as distinct from the contract of works, or independent contracting, i.e. the *locatio conductio operis.*

INTRODUCTION

1.1 Origins

The contract of employment goes back more than 2,000 years and is vested in the law of contract. South African contract law is a modernised version of Roman-Dutch law, with some English legal influence.

In its broadest definition, a contract is an agreement between two or more parties entered into with the intention of creating one or more legal obligations. Contract law provides for an all important legal framework within which persons can transact commercially and exchange resources, secure in the knowledge that the law will uphold their agreement and enforce this when necessary to do so, for instance in the event of a breach of contract. The law of contract is the foundation of private enterprise and business in South Africa, and regulates these in the interest of all parties. Imagine the ensuing societal catastrophe should the terms and conditions of contracts become unenforceable, or largely unenforceable, for whatever reason?

It serves to be mentioned that *pacta sunt servanda,* reasonableness and good faith, provide the cornerstones of the law of contract. The principle of *pacta sunt servanda* literally means "agreements must be kept". When two parties voluntarily and knowingly enter into a contract, the terms of that contract must be upheld by both parties. The courts will also, in adjudicating on the enforceability of contracts, take into account the aforementioned three principles in addition to constitutional values, the public interest, and the conciliatory concept of ubuntu.

The Supreme Court of Appeal in *Brisley v Drotsky* 2002(4) SA 1 (SCA), in deciding that a contract that has been entered into freely must be enforced, held as follows:

> *"What is evident is that neither the Constitution nor the value system it embodies give the courts a general jurisdiction to invalidate contracts on the basis of traditionally perceived notions of unjustness or to determine their enforceability on the basis of imprecise notions of good faith. On the contrary, the Constitutional values of dignity and equality and freedom require that the courts approach their task of striking down contracts or declining to enforce them with perceptive restraint. One of the reasons, as Davis, J has pointed out, is that contractual autonomy informs also the Constitutional value of dignity."* (Cameron, J.A.)

1.2 Employer and Employee: Contractual Inter-Dependency

Work and the provision of services in order to make a living is a fundamental human activity, and the employment relationship entails the provision of work or services in exchange for reward in cash or kind.

The employment contract establishes the fundamentals of the relationship between employee and employer, irrespective of how humble and seemingly insignificant, or dynamic, specialised and highly paid, the nature of the job is. It is also the point of departure for the entire system of labour relations law and rules, and such rules depend solely on there being a contract of employment in place.

Employment and labour law consists of a set of rules emanating from both the common law as well as statute. Legislation was introduced in the public interest in order to counter-balance the inherent power of an employer vis-à-vis the employee, and in order to protect the latter from exploitation. In this country, comprehensive post-1994 labour legislation was introduced not only to protect the new constitutional rights and freedoms of employees, but also to redress historical power imbalances. The ambit, extent and nature of the common law contract of employment was singularly insufficient to promote the desired protection in response to unfettered managerial control and authenticity, as well as the power of capital.

The objective of this book, in addition to highlighting the importance and relevance of contracts in daily life, is to provide a practical guide for the drafting, conclusion and termination of such contracts, inclusive of the contractual considerations to be kept in mind. It is not intended to be an academic or exhaustive reference work.

1.3 The Employment Contract as a Commercial Agreement

An employment contract is an agreement between an employer and an employee that regulates the terms and conditions of employment between the parties. A valid contract is entered into as soon as the parties are in agreement on the nature of the job, the wage, and duration of the work to be provided. One of the crucial elements is the agreement to exchange services in return for money or value.

A contract comes into existence in a voluntary manner and is concluded between an employer and an individual employee. The contract of employment does not need to be in writing - indeed verbal contracts are common - however creating it in a written format will provide for legal certainty, and will further ensure that there is clarity on the terms and conditions thereof, reducing the chances of opportunistic interpretations and disputes.

In modern employment relations and human resource management, the contract of employment ("*letter of appointment*") is considered to be a vital document, to be set out in writing, and is the source of the original intention and purpose of the parties. This contract is the cornerstone of the employment relationship, and inevitably, all future questions and answers related to the relationship will by necessity be channelled back to its contents.

Although it may seem obvious that the contract of employment contains the terms and conditions specifically offered or agreed to between the parties, inclusive of those automatically included by law, such contract can never provide, and in fact is not intended, to cover all eventualities.

The employer's customs and practices, including implied terms or unwritten understandings, will usually form part and parcel of a contract of employment.

As noted above, the contract will state what the employee will receive in terms of salary in return for the work to be performed, and how such work will be performed. It will also provide for essential issues immediately within the decision-making ambit of the parties, and should not dwell on custom and practice, which is implied into the contract in any event.

There are essentially two types of employment contracts, i.e. for permanent or for temporary duration purposes, and permutations of these contract forms exist for specific purposes.

1.4 The Employee

All categories of employees will have contracts of employment, and are appointed in terms of the provisions of such contracts of employment, whether these are concluded orally or in writing. This means that even part-time of temporary staff will have a contract, whether or not they:

- have a fixed employment period;
- only work one day a week;
- only work every weekend; or
- only work half day.

To sum up, an employment contract is a voluntary agreement between an employer and the employee, in which the employee undertakes to render personal services, under the control and authority of the employer, to such employer in return for determined remuneration in money or value.

OVERVIEW

This book deals with the employment contract in South Africa and the importance of this document as the foundation of the commercial relationship between the employee and the employer.

It begins by describing the nature and relevance of the contract of employment (as distinct from independent contracting), the essential components and conclusion of the contract, the legislative framework and aspects related to breaches of the contract, as well as repudiation and the termination of the contract.

The book then proceeds to discuss employment issues as they relate to the 'new normal', including topics such as Remote and Hybrid Working, and the effect this has had on managerial control and authority.

The book is intended to provide practical assistance and information to the entrepreneur, business owner, front-line manager, trade union representative and official, who is, no matter how experienced, always in need of a quick reference guide and source of knowledge.

HOW TO USE THIS BOOK?

1. Chapters 1 to 5 deal with the contract of employment, and the nuts and bolts of what the employment relationship consists of. In order to place the contract of employment in the proper context and understand the consequences as well as the implications of the conclusion of such a contract, these chapters need to be read and understood especially in respect of practical implementation and the monitoring of steps and measures. Chapters 6 to 8 are aimed at demystifying the complexities of breaches of a contract of employment and available remedies.

2. The sample (Toolkit) documentation at the end of the book consists of examples of contracts, policies, procedures, strategy guidelines and conditions of employment, which should provide for a handy point of departure in order to draft fresh contracts, as well as for the customisation of, and amendment to, existing contracts and letters of appointment.

3. The Toolkit sample contracts are intended to be user-friendly, and have been designed to avoid over legalistic drafting and terminology; they lend themselves to easy adaption and customisation. A significant number of important subjects are dealt with in this Toolkit, and some will be of more importance than others, depending on the nature of the employer's enterprise and specific circumstances.

4. In drafting new or amending existing contracts and letters of appointment, there will naturally be a process of cross-reference between Chapters 1 to 8 of the book, as well as the contents of the Toolkit.

5. The following diagram, which deals with the termination of a contract of employment, should serve to illustrate the interplay between the contents of the chapters in the book and the Toolkit documents:

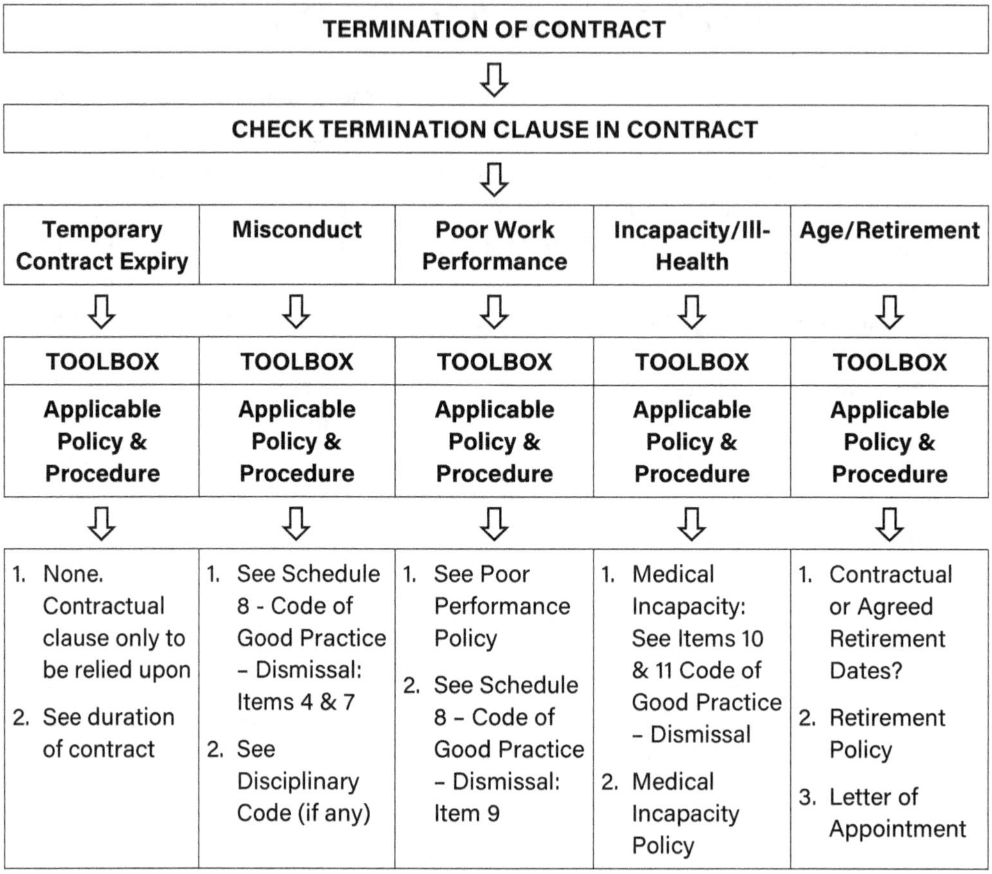

TERMINATION OF CONTRACT

⇩

CHECK TERMINATION CLAUSE IN CONTRACT

⇩

Temporary Contract Expiry	**Misconduct**	**Poor Work Performance**	**Incapacity/Ill-Health**	**Age/Retirement**
⇩	⇩	⇩	⇩	⇩
TOOLBOX	**TOOLBOX**	**TOOLBOX**	**TOOLBOX**	**TOOLBOX**
Applicable Policy & Procedure	**Applicable Policy & Procedure**	**Applicable Policy & Procedure**	**Applicable Policy & Procedure**	**Applicable Policy & Procedure**
⇩	⇩	⇩	⇩	⇩
1. None. Contractual clause only to be relied upon 2. See duration of contract	1. See Schedule 8 - Code of Good Practice - Dismissal: Items 4 & 7 2. See Disciplinary Code (if any)	1. See Poor Performance Policy 2. See Schedule 8 – Code of Good Practice – Dismissal: Item 9	1. Medical Incapacity: See Items 10 & 11 Code of Good Practice – Dismissal 2. Medical Incapacity Policy	1. Contractual or Agreed Retirement Dates? 2. Retirement Policy 3. Letter of Appointment

Figure 1.1: Interplay between chapters and toolkits

CHAPTER 2

IDENTIFYING THE PARTIES TO THE CONTRACT

Human beings are, by nature, inclined to search for the proverbial "lower hanging fruit", which can be secured with relative ease and little effort. In the employment relationship, the equivalent can be described as the passive and uncomplaining employee. So why should the employer be burdened with a complicated contract of employment with all sorts of impediments, interferences and conditions? The perennial search for a Roman Law contract that originated 2,000 years ago, the locatio conductio operis, has just commenced!

2.1 Introduction

The control and authority of the employer over the employee, whether or not such control is by means of indirect, remote or non-tangible means, provides for the hallmark of the contract of employment and indeed, the employment relationship.

As explained in Chapter 1, the contract of employment may be described as an agreement between an employer and an employee for work to be done in return for some form of remuneration. In performing such work, the employee places him or herself under the control, supervision and authority of their employer.

The element of 'control and authority' is an important and distinguishing feature. In the absence of this, an entirely different relationship, i.e. that of an independent contractor, may come into existence. The latter is not a contract of employment, although it also entails the provision of work or services. The independent contractor is not regarded as an employee under South African labour legislation, and nor can he or she be regarded as the true agent or partner in a business.

People such as doctors, dentists, lawyers, accountants, electricians, plumbers, contractors and sub-contractors who are in an independent trade, business or profession in which they offer their services to other instances or businesses, are generally regarded as independent contractors.

However, whether these people are independent contractors or employees depends on the facts of each case. The general rule is that an individual is an independent contractor if the payer has the right to control or direct only the result of the work, and not what will be done and how it will be done. The earnings of an independent contractor are also not subject to monthly payroll taxes by the business receiving the services, and these people are regarded as self-employed.

The distinction between an employee and an independent contractor is of critical importance because different legal consequences flow from these different types of contracts.

2.2 **Employee vs. Independent Contractor**

An 'employee' is defined in South African labour legislation as:

> *"(a) any person, excluding an independent contractor, who works for another person or for the State, and who receives, or is entitled to receive any remuneration; and*
>
> *(b) any other person who in any manner assists in carrying on or conducting the business of an employer." (Section 1 of the Basic Conditions of Employment Act 75 of 1997 (BCEA)).*

In theory, the distinction between an employee and an independent contractor will more than likely be obvious and not difficult to draw. In practice, however, and sometimes as a result of 'disguised employment', the differences can become complicated, with the result that the South African courts have developed various tests to assist in distinguishing the one from the other.

Some employers will, for obvious reasons, prefer to predominantly employ 'independent contractors' because such persons fall outside of the protective net of labour legislation, which provides for less onerous management of the relationship.

The International Labour Organisation's (ILO) recommendations concerning the Employment Relationship (Rec. 198 of 2006) state that a *"disguised employment occurs when the employer treats an individual as other than an employee in a manner that hides his or her true legal status as an employee".*

The "Code of Practice: Who is an Employee" to the Labour Relations Act 66 of 1995 (LRA) acknowledges the real problem of opportunistic, if not unscrupulous, instances of an employment relationship being disguised as an 'independent contractor' relationship. This is designed to circumvent, if not nullify, the minimum standards which have been put in place by labour legislation to protect employees. The same level of protection and oversight is not afforded to independent contractors.

Section 200A of the LRA and section 83A of the BCEA have been enacted as a direct response to the problems posed by disguised employment. A rebuttable presumption (for employers) was introduced, which means that, if triggered, a person so employed is presumed to be an employee and a burden will be on the employer to prove that the person is in fact not an employee. Section 83A of the BCEA unequivocally provides for the following:

"Presumption as to who is an Employee –

1. *A person who works for, or provides services to, another person is an employee if –*
   - *(a) his or her manner or hours of work are subject to control or direction;*
   - *(b) he or she forms part of the employer's organisation;*
   - *(c) he or she has worked for the other person for at least 40 hours per month over the previous three months;*
   - *(d) he or she is economically dependent on the other person;*
   - *(e) he or she is provided with his or her tools or work equipment; or*
   - *(f) he or she only works for, or renders service to, one person.*
2. *If one of these factors is present, the person is presumed to be an employee until the employer proves that he or she is not".*

The aforementioned section 83A (promulgated in 2020) has largely disposed of the debates surrounding the distinction between real, genuine employment and independent contractors providing services.

Nevertheless, The Code of Practice referred to above sets out guidelines for determining who is an employee. The courts have frequently held that the classification of these contracts is a matter of substance, not merely of form.

What this means is the fact that the parties have given their contract a specific label, for example "XXX", is not conclusive. The true nature of the contract is to be ascertained from circumstantial evidence. Such investigations are sometimes referred to as the "Dominant Impression" or "Reality" tests, and are also prominent in international labour law developments, where the fine line between employment and independent contracting is continuously shifting, in order to test new boundaries.

In the case of an employment relationship (as distinct from agency), the employee is an integral part of the organisation and is required to:

- render personal services;
- place himself or herself under the employer's control and authority; and
- comply with rules and regulations, inclusive of conduct and disciplinary standards.

In addition, the employee will (to a large extent) be economically dependent on the employer.

This distinction between these types of contracts can be summed up by means of the following table:

Table 2.1: Employment contract vs. Independent contractor

EMPLOYMENT CONTRACT	INDEPENDENT CONTRACTOR
The rendering of personal services.	The production of a specified service or the production of a certain specified result.
Employees render services at the discretion and behest of the employer.	Independent contractor is not obliged to perform work personally (unless otherwise agreed).
Employer may decide whether it elects to have employee render service.	Independent contractor is bound to perform specified work or produce a specified result within a specified or reasonable time, at own discretion.
Employee obliged to obey lawful instructions regarding work to be done and manner in which it is to be done.	Independent contractor is not obliged to obey instructions regarding manner in which task is to be performed.
Contract terminated by the death of the employee.	Contract not terminated by the death of the contractor.
Employment terminates on completion of agreed period (fixed-term contract).	Contract terminates on completion of the specified work or production of the specified result.

For a sample Independent Contractor's Agreement, refer to the Toolkit section in this book.

2.3 **Classification of Employees**

2.3.1 **Introduction**

The statutory definition of "employee" makes no distinction between permanent, casual, temporary or probationary employees, and senior managerial employees and directors are not excluded from such definition. All are eligible for protection against unacceptable employment conditions, unfair labour practices and non-compliant dismissals.

In section 3 of the BCEA State security employees, as well as unpaid volunteers working for a charitable purpose are excluded. In addition some employees in respect of specified conditions of employment are also excluded (those earning above a statutory threshold), e.g. the automatic statutory right to be compensated for planned overtime work. There is nothing however, preventing the employee (earning above the statutory threshold) from negotiating and demanding from the employer some additional payment for overtime worked, when having been instructed to do so by the employer.

Employees working for an employer for less than 24 hours per month are also excluded from the BCEA, but such employees are entitled to the protective mechanisms of the LRA and the EEA.

2.3.2 Permanent employees

These are employees appointed on a permanent or 'indefinite' basis with the expectation that employment will continue with the fullness of time, or at least until the retirement or death of the employee. The contract can also end by the giving of notice by either party, for material breach, or in the event that the contract of employment is terminated for reasons related to misconduct, incapacity, or retrenchment.

2.3.3 Temporary employees ('casual staff')

In this form of employment, at least in the initial stages, the parties are aware and agree that the employment relationship is for a temporary, finite period of time and that there can or should be no expectation of long-term employment.

The intention is for the employment relationship to continue for as long as the employee's services are required, which normally provides an attractive option for the employer who chooses not to be burdened by long-term employment obligations. The longer the period of service, the more "rights", implied or otherwise, accrue for the employee.

No matter how brief the fixed period of employment, the parties are still reciprocally bound by a contract of employment and the notice provisions of the BCEA, which means that temporary or casual employees are entitled to at least one weeks' notice of termination during the first six months' service, two weeks during the second six months' service, and a minimum of four weeks' notice after that.

Temporary employees may also colloquially be referred to as *"casual employees"*, i.e. those persons who tender their services on a daily basis, often as general labourers, from the street corners of our towns and cities. Albeit for a very short period, an employment contract (typically a verbal one) comes into being for the duration of the services tendered by the casual employee. Naturally, and as a result of the tenuous and short term work offered, as well as practicalities, these employees have limited access to the protection of labour laws.

All employees, regardless of category, are in principle entitled to statutory protection, provided that an employment contract exists. However, employees who work for less than 24 hours per month are not entitled to most of the employment conditions prescribed by the BCEA.

'Temporary', 'casual', 'fixed-term' or 'project-based' contracts of employment provide for the automatic cessation of the employment relationship upon expiry of a specified time period or event, and no consequences attach to its non-renewal, provided that it is in fact not renewed. The expiry of the time periods provided for in these contracts does not constitute dismissal.

2.3.4 Employees employed on a project basis

Employment on a fixed-term or project basis is normally a feature of the civil engineering, building and construction industry, where the employee is engaged for a particular period, for a phase of the project, or for the completion of the entire works, e.g. the building of a road, dam, railway, house or bridge.

The understanding at the conclusion of the employment contract is that the latter ceases to exist by operation of law, i.e. the employment relationship ends contractually and expires upon the completion of the project or works.

Complications arise when the parties agree implicitly, or more often tacitly, to renew the fixed-term contract of employment and to continue "as is". The employee inevitably ends up in a comfort zone, expecting further 'contractual renewals', with the result being that the relationship is swiftly converted, for all practical purposes and intent, to a permanent contract of employment. The cessation of the temporary contract of employment, in terms of expiry, will not constitute a dismissal, therefore the unfair dismissal provisions and jurisdiction of the LRA will not be applicable, as a dismissal is a precondition for such jurisdiction. However, the pitfalls of contract renewals alluded to hereinabove provide for real complications in terms of the provisions of section 186 of the LRA:

"Meaning of dismissal and unfair labour practice

(1) 'Dismissal' means that –

(a) an employer has terminated employment with or without notice;

(b) an employee employed in terms of a fixed-term contract of employment reasonably expect the employer -

(i) to renew a fixed-term contract of employment on the same or similar terms but the employer offered to renew it on less favourable terms, or did not renew it; or

(ii) to retain the employee in employment on an indefinite basis but otherwise

on the same or similar terms as the fixed-term contract, but the employer offered to retain the employee *on less favourable terms, or did not offer to retain the employee".*

2.4 Other Categories of Employees

2.4.1 Probationary employees

Newly appointed employees are sometimes required to perform a period of probation during which their capacity, abilities and skills are assessed and evaluated by the employer, normally over a period of three to six months. Employers should carefully consider whether it is in their interests to embark on a probationary policy in contracts of employment, as these could end up being highly onerous and unproductive exercises. This is because probationary employees have the same terms, conditions and protections as other employees, and there are no attenuated or expedited dismissal procedures applicable in South Africa, as is the case in most other comparable jurisdictions.

Item 8 of the LRA's 'Code of Good Practice – Dismissal' (see Toolkit) contains detailed guidelines, procedures and steps to be taken by employers in respect of probationary employees, as discussed below.

In the case of probationary employees, the opportunities for counselling and warnings related to, for instance, sub-standard work, are limited by the shorter period of service, and it is recognised that the relationship could be considered to be precarious in its early and initial stages.

Probationary employees are obviously and in principle entitled to fair treatment, but they cannot lay claim to the same degree of security of tenure as other longer serving employees.

The extension of probationary periods is a matter for agreement between the parties, and should only be resorted to under exceptional circumstances and not as an action to avoid the inevitable termination of employment.

There is a misconception held by some that a probationary clause in the contract of employment can be beneficial and of assistance to employers in the event of termination of employment. However, as can be seen from the above, this is often no more than an illusion, and clauses dealing with probationary periods must be treated with the necessary caution and circumspection.

2.4.2 Seasonal employees

These contracts of employment are prevalent in the agricultural, farming, fishing and food processing industries, and the employment of seasonal employees is comparable to temporary or project-based employment relationships. These contracts normally have, in common with construction norms, the stipulation that cessation of work as a result of, for instance, inclement weather, will mean that there will be no payment in respect of such downtime. Seasonal workers can also only expect to be paid for work actually performed, and the interruption of harvesting could mean the implementation of the "no-work-no-pay" principle, unless there is agreement to the contrary.

The BCEA does not define the term 'seasonal employee', but section 84 (Duration of Employment) gives protection to such employees by providing that all periods of previous employment with the same employer must be taken into account when determining the length of the employee's service (unless there is a break in employment of longer than one year). This protects seasonal employees in two important ways, i.e.:

- it ensures that seasonal employees who are retrenched and re-employed within one year remain entitled to severance pay in respect of their full period of service; and
- it reinforces the entitlement of seasonal employees' to rights which depend on length of service such as annual leave, sick leave, family responsibility leave and notice of termination.

A sample Contract of Employment for Seasonal Workers is provided in the Toolkit section.

2.4.3 Temporary employment services (labour broking)

Section 82 of the BCEA and 198 of the LRA deals extensively with the rights of the parties in the event of temporary staff being provided by labour brokers, however this goes beyond the scope of this book. Employers making extensive use of the services of temporary employees are normally adequately covered in agreements with labour brokers, and should have a separate Temporary Employment Service (TES) policy in this regard.

Although the TES is regarded as the employer of an employee whose services it provides to a client, such employee becomes the employee of the client after a period of three months' employment. The TES and the client will be jointly and severally bound as far as the employee is concerned if the TES does not comply with all employment obligations as an employer, or in the event of an unfair dismissal claim.

2.4.4 Age and retirement

There is no statutory retirement age applicable to employees, and the question often, if not increasingly, arises as to when employees should retire, and if and when employers can compel older employees to retire. The employer cannot just suddenly and unilaterally decide that an older employee must "be put out to pasture" in the absence of due process. A point of departure is that the employer should have a clear policy in respect of its retirement age or the retirement age could be agreed upon between the parties in the contract of employment, or in a separate written undertaking. In the absence of an agreed retirement age, an employer may retire an employee who has reached the retirement age that is the norm, i.e. in accordance with the custom and practice of that employer. Parties normally agree in the employment contract on a retirement age, or often agree that the retirement age will be as per company policy or the rules of a particular retirement fund.

Section 187 of the LRA (Automatically Unfair Dismissals) provides for a general prohibition against any discriminatory practices, inclusive of discrimination on the basis of age, but does provide that *"a dismissal based on age is fair if the employee has reached the normal or agreed retirement age for persons employed in that capacity".* Legal complications can arise for the unsuspecting employer if there was no provision or agreement in respect of the "normal or agreed age", and the employee needs to "be retired".

It is therefore incumbent on the employer to include and to state in the contract of employment as to what the retirement age is, and that the contract will automatically expire or cease by the operation of law, which does not constitute a dismissal.

The employer's retirement policy and procedure should ensure that possible potentially costly mistakes are minimised, and preferably eliminated, and should provide for a procedure to be followed when the employee is retired from employment. (For a sample Retirement Policy see the Toolkit section).

In the event of non-compliance with section 187(2)(b), i.e. in the absence of: (a) an agreed retirement age, or (b) a 'normal retirement age' as per the employer's retirement policy, or past custom and practice, the employer will have a steep hill to climb to defend what should be a fairly straightforward claim of automatic (unfair) dismissal, which could result in 24 months' compensation or a reinstatement of the employee with retrospective back pay.

The mere fact that an employee is allowed to work beyond normal retirement age does not preclude the employer from requesting that employee to retire at any stage after that, and provided that the correct procedures in place have been followed, this will not constitute a dismissal. In such cases, employees are entitled to be consulted and advised on their exit from employment.

Based on the above, it is advisable for employers to ensure that they include an agreed retirement age when concluding contracts of employment. Employers should also bear in mind that if they are relying on the concept of "normal" retirement age, they must ensure that such a norm has been ongoing and that such norm has been applied consistently. Should an employer be unable to show that it retired an employee based on the agreed or normal retirement age, the dismissal does not enjoy the prohibited ground and falls outside the section 187(2)(b) defence, with sometimes disastrous consequences for the employer.

2.4.5 **Peripheral employees**

The validity of contracts of employment concluded in spite of statutory or other prohibitions must be interpreted in the light of the Constitution of the Republic of South Africa, 1996 (the Constitution).

Section 23 of the Constitution provides that, *"Everyone has the right to fair labour practices"*, irrespective of nationality and citizenship. The LRA applies to employees and employers falling under the jurisdiction of the South African courts, and accordingly millions of foreign nationals employed within South Africa's borders fall within the scope of labour legislation. Whereas a contract of employment concluded for unlawful or nefarious purposes will not be enforceable, this needs to be distinguished from contracts that provide for the performance of legal work, but which are, for instance, invalid for want of statutory compliance, e.g. immigration requirements and work permit legislation, taking into account all applicable regulations.

Accordingly, foreign workers employed without the necessary compliance documentation still fall within the ambit of labour legislation.

Employees working for less than 24 hours per month for an employer as well as those persons providing services in terms of 'algorithmic employment' are also considered to be peripheral employees.

2.4.6 **Insolvency**

In the event of the insolvency or liquidation of the employer, contracts of employment terminate automatically and employees become preferred creditors.

Section 197A of the LRA provides for the transfer of a contract of employment in circumstances of involuntary insolvency, when an insolvent company is transferred to a new owner. The new employer is then automatically substituted in the place of the old employer, in respect of all contracts of employment in existence immediately before insolvency.

However, in the event of the employer applying for voluntary sequestration or liquidation, the consequent termination of contracts of employment will constitute dismissals if there is no new employer.

2.4.7 Applicants for employment and deemed employees

Naturally, an employment relationship will usually only commence when the parties conclude a contract of employment. There are two exceptions to this principle, both of which are created by statute.

First, the Employment Equity Act 55 of 1998 ("the EEA") prohibits the direct or indirect unfair discrimination against employees and applicants for employment on various grounds. The LRA and the BCEA protect both employees and persons seeking employment against discrimination, and for exercising rights conferred by those Acts.

Secondly, there is a presumption of employment created by the LRA and the BCEA in certain circumstances, for example the provisions of sections 200A (LRA) and 83A (BCEA) respectively. This may, therefore, also result in parties being deemed to be employers and employees (even though the contract may formally state that their relationship is not one of employment, labelling the contract as something else).

Subject to these exceptions, the employment contract brings into being an employment relationship that is regulated by an extensive legislative framework, not only in this country, but in most constitutional democracies worldwide.

2.4.8 Atypical employees or 'gig' employees

Employment relations and the labour market today is drastically different to 20 years ago. The fourth industrial revolution, as well as related socio-economic and political circumstances, has led to the development of a further category of employment and the provision of services, referred to as a gig labour economy. This category covers a significant variety of work permutations mostly characterised by job flexibility, mobility, little security and minimal direct employer control. The term "gig" originates from the music sector, being a colloquial reference to a service or a job that lasts for a short or fixed period.

Atypical forms of work include part timers, temporary assignments, freelancers, job sharing, work from home (WFH) and remote working, as well as the work of unpaid spouses or family members in business together. It is difficult to identify and describe atypical forms of employment, and most lack statutory regulation by intent or design. A related class of work is referred to as "ghost work", which anthropologist Mary L. Gray called "the invisible labor that powers technological platforms".

"Ghost work" has also been defined as work that can be done remotely, with internet access, on a contract basis. This is a Silicon Valley-type, mostly invisible, workforce made up of those who treat it as a full time job and those who perform it on a casual basis. What these atypical workers have in common is relatively unregulated employment, with little statutory interference and employer obligations.

Once again, the parameters of the control aspect in the contract of employment are being tested, with the difference between "pay" and "control" becoming increasingly blurred.

These atypical or gig "employees" cannot easily be defined as employees or independent contractors, and could well occupy a space between the aforementioned forms of employment or services. For instance, they may not be subject to employment taxes, but their income can derive from only one entity, and a contract of employment might never be concluded. In addition they are self-employed, not reliant on statutory protections, and will quite possibly never meet their "employer" in person.

The existing model of work which consists of common law principles and legislative employment structures does not always reflect the practical, true nature of employment arrangements. This is nothing new as the atypical employees have outnumbered the traditional "8 to 5" permanent employees in recent times. As a result, the practical impact of employment legislation which was drafted largely with typical employment in mind has become compromised.

The development of another regulatory system of employment relations is a reality in the context of the fourth industrial revolution "4IR", which is changing the basis of traditional work, inclusive of the employer's control and authority.

"4IR" has been described as "the fourth major industrial era since the initial Industrial Revolution of the 18th century. It is characterized by a fusion of technologies that is blurring the lines between the physical, digital, and biological spheres, collectively referred to as cyber-physical systems. It is marked by emerging technology breakthroughs in a number of fields..." (Wikipedia date unknown https://en.wikipedia.org/wiki/Fourth_Industrial_Revolution)

The diagram on page 20 illustrates The Hybrid Provision of Employment and Services.

For the purposes of this chapter, reference should be made to the Contracts of Employment as well as the Independent Contractor's Agreement contained in the Toolkit.

NOTES ON PROVISION OF HYBRID EMPLOYMENT AND SERVICES CHART

1. The terms 'temporary employees', 'casual workers', 'part-time employees' and 'contract workers' are often used interchangeably, and these workers are generally known as 'temporary employees'. These "on demand" workers, WFH and "platform" or "intermediary employees" are far greater in number than the normal permanent or temporary employees, employees which labour legislation sets out to protect. They generally work fewer hours compared to permanent employees. They are also often excluded from additional employment benefits such as medical aid and pension funds and provide for little in respect of contingent liability.

2. The statutory definition of 'employee' however, does not differentiate between different categories of employee. All categories of employees are included in the definition of an 'employee' and therefore qualify for protection under labour law statutes.

3. Increasingly the control and authority element of the contract of employment is being inadvertently challenged, as stated elsewhere in this book. Most employers, for obvious reasons, prefer to have employees without long term obligations and contingent liability for instance, severance money and dismissal legal costs. Work in the modern economy has become casualised outsourced and broken apart. Such employees are being managed by and through data and a system of algorithmic management*.

4. Currently many platform companies (e.g. Uber) operate in an environment in which the triangular relationship between the platform, customer and employee is relatively far removed from the 'employer'. The indispensible element of control and authority is becoming a victim of developments.

   * 'Algorithmic management' is described as a diverse set of technological tools and techniques to remotely manage work forces, relying on data collection and surveillance of workers to enable automated or semi-automated decision making.

Figure 2.1: Hybrid Provision of Employment and Services

CHAPTER 3

THE LEGISLATIVE FRAMEWORK

Laws, decrees, edicts, canons, writs and statutory directives are societal instruments that are intended to curb and regulate the conduct of people as well as to prevent mischief, for the "better of all" and in the public interest. In this chapter, the restraining forces and salutary consequences of legislation and acts of parliament or "permanent laws' are dealt with in the context of employment, and in particular the contract of employment.

3.1 Introduction

3.1.1 The contract of employment has been described as an agreement between an employer and employee, where the latter places him or herself under the control and authority of the employer, in order to render services in exchange for remuneration of any kind.

3.1.2 As stated hereinabove, the employer, as an owner of the means of production, is in a far superior bargaining position viz-a-viz the employee, because of the elements of control and authority, payment of remuneration, and the right of dismissal. These are incredibly powerful, contractual forces at work, and the status quo has remained relatively intact, irrespective of paternalistic legislation aimed at trying to narrow this imbalance, internationally as well as locally.

3.1.3 Kahn-Freund pronounced as follows:

"The relations between and employer and an isolated employee or worker is typically a relation between a bearer of power and one who is not a bearer of power. The main object of labour law has been and ... will always be, to be a countervailing force to counteract the inequality of bargaining power which is inherent and must be inherent in the employment relationship."

3.2 Primary Statutes

The principal labour statutes in South Africa - the Labour Relations Act 66 of 1995 (LRA), the Employment Equity Act 55 of 998 (EEA), and the Basic

Conditions of Employment Act 75 of 1997 (BCEA) - are all intended to give effect to the general constitutional right to fair employment practices, in order to set and stabilise terms and conditions of employment in the public interest and for the common good, illustrated as follows:

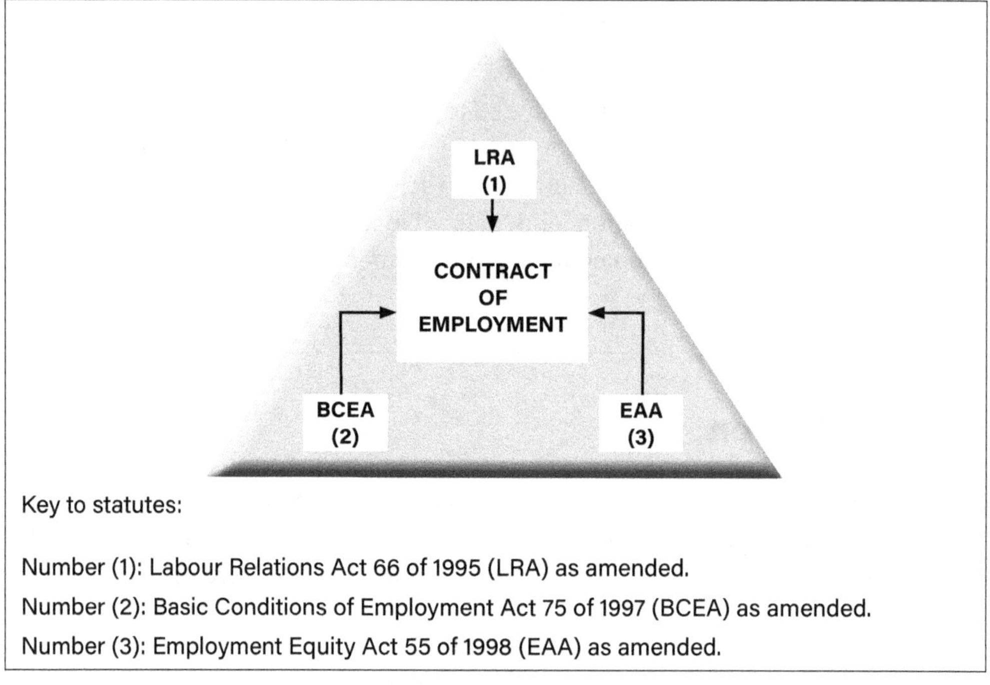

Figure 3.1: Labour Legislation Diagram - Primary Statutes

3.2.1 Further legislation which has an impact on the employment relationship, as well as on the contract of employment, are the following Acts:

- Occupational Health and Safety Act 85 of 1993 as amended.
- Unemployment Insurance Act 63 of 2001 as amended.
- Mine Health and Safety Act 29 of 1996 as amended.
- Protection of Personal Information Act 4 of 2013 as amended.
- Protected Disclosures Act 26 of 2000 as amended.
- Promotion of Equality and Prevention of Unfair Discrimination Act 4 of 2000 as amended.
- Promotion of Administrative Justice Act 3 of 2000 as amended.
- The Public Service Act 103 of 1994 as amended.
- BCEA Sectoral Determinations.

- Regulation of Interception of Communications and Provision of Communication Related Information Act 70 of 2002 as amended.
- The National Health Act 61 of 2003 as amended.
- Conventional Penalties Act 15 of 1962 as amended.
- Promotion of Access to Information Act, no. 2 of 2000.

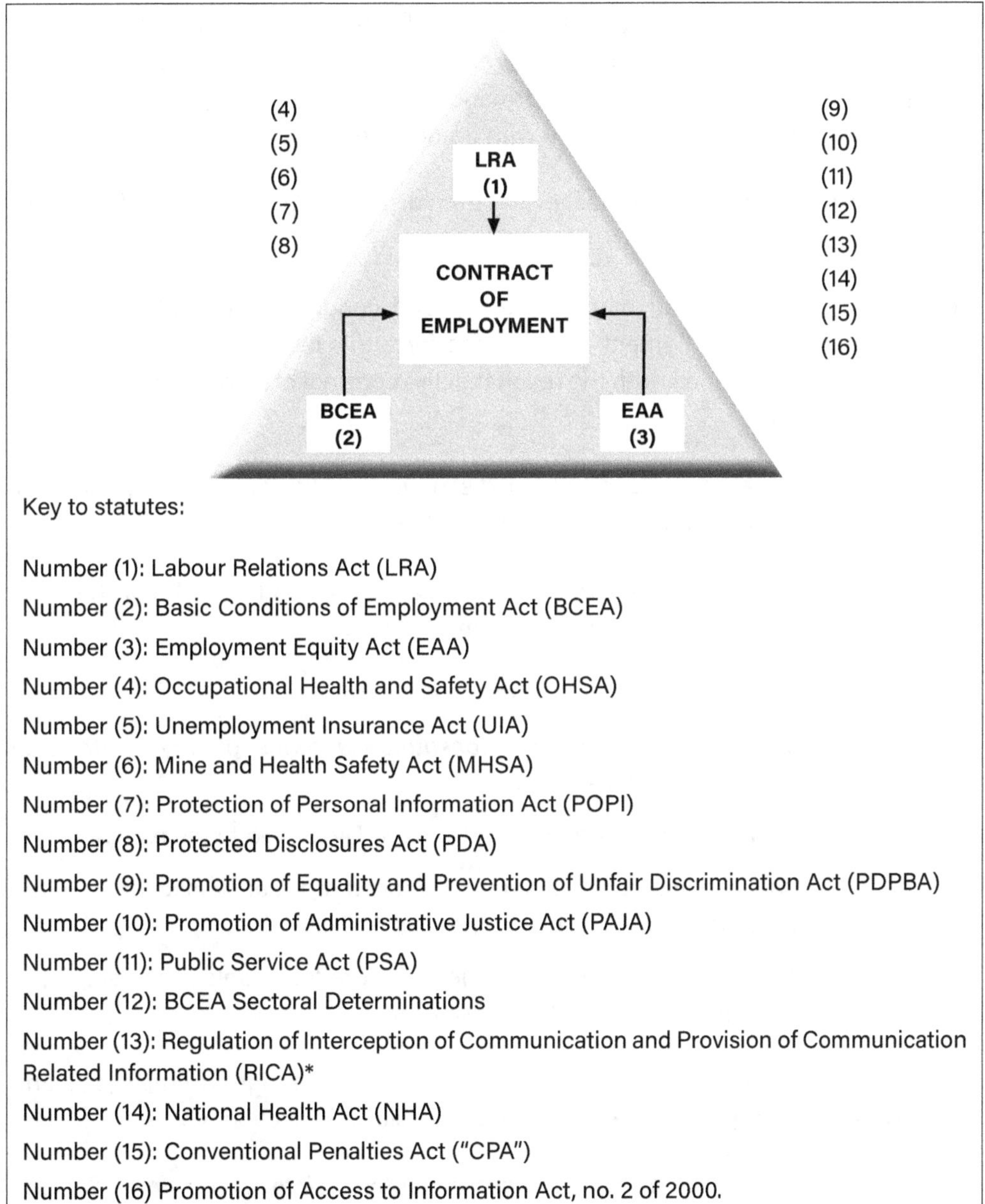

Key to statutes:

Number (1): Labour Relations Act (LRA)
Number (2): Basic Conditions of Employment Act (BCEA)
Number (3): Employment Equity Act (EAA)
Number (4): Occupational Health and Safety Act (OHSA)
Number (5): Unemployment Insurance Act (UIA)
Number (6): Mine and Health Safety Act (MHSA)
Number (7): Protection of Personal Information Act (POPI)
Number (8): Protected Disclosures Act (PDA)
Number (9): Promotion of Equality and Prevention of Unfair Discrimination Act (PDPBA)
Number (10): Promotion of Administrative Justice Act (PAJA)
Number (11): Public Service Act (PSA)
Number (12): BCEA Sectoral Determinations
Number (13): Regulation of Interception of Communication and Provision of Communication Related Information (RICA)*
Number (14): National Health Act (NHA)
Number (15): Conventional Penalties Act ("CPA")
Number (16) Promotion of Access to Information Act, no. 2 of 2000.

Figure 3.2: Labour Legislation Diagram – All the Statutes

*In the matter of *Amabhungane Centre for Investigative Journalism NPC and Another v Minister of Justice and Correctional Services and Others* (CCT278/19 & CCT279/19), the Constitutional Court, (in repealing RICA) acknowledged the constitutional importance of the right to privacy, which is tied to dignity, thereby confirming that the RICA was unconstitutional. Amongst other matters, RICA failed to provide adequate safeguards to protect the right to privacy, as buttressed by the rights of access to courts, freedom of expression and the media, inclusive of legal privilege. The effect of this important judgment has suspended the invalidity of RICA until 2023 for Parliament to revise the Act, except in respect of the issues of notification of post surveillance, and confidentiality for information shared with legal practitioners and journalists, which have been amended with immediate effect.

3.2.2 The LRA regulates all disputes arising from dismissals and alleged unfair labour practices.

The BCEA provides for minimum terms and conditions of employment, and no contract of employment may provide for terms less favourable than those prescribed conditions, with the result that the contract of employment is directly impacted upon.

Disputes concerning alleged unfair discrimination are governed by the EEA, save for the LRA's jurisdiction in respect of unfair discriminations.

3.2.3 Section 4 of the BCEA states the following to ensure that contracts of employment are not designed to circumvent the provisions of the Act:

"4 Inclusion of provisions in contracts of employment

A basic condition of employment constitutes a terms of any contract of employment except to the extent that –

(a) any other law provides a term that is more favourable to the employee;

(b) the basic condition of employment has been replaced, varied, or excluded in accordance with the provisions of this Act; or

(c) a term of the contract of employment is more favourable to the employee than the basic condition of employment."

In addition to the above, section 5 of the LRA (Protection of employees and persons seeking employment) provides as follows in section 5(4):

"A provision in any contract, whether entered into before or after the commencement of this Act, that directly or indirectly contradicts or limits any

provision of section 4 ("freedom of association"), or this section is invalid, unless the contractual provision is permitted by this Act."

3.2.4 The LRA, as a measure to regulate fair employment practices, provides as follows in section 185:

"185 Right not to be unfairly dismissed or subjected to unfair labour practice

Every employee has the right not to be-

(a) Unfairly dismissed; and

(b) Subjected to unfair labour practice"

3.2.5 The LRA provides for a dynamic piece of legislation designed to regulate fundamental individual rights and to provide a framework within which employers, employees and trade unions can bargain collectively to determine wages and conditions of employment, in accordance with the principles of "industrial democracy".

3.2.6 Section 2 of the LRA excludes specific categories of persons from the ambit of the Act in order to avoid a conflict of interest in the national interest, i.e. members of the SADF, the National Intelligence Agency, and the South African Secret Service (often referred to as "soldiers, spooks and spies"). Section 3 of the BCEA excludes 'spooks and spies' and unpaid volunteers providing services for a charitable purpose. Persons employed on vessels at sea are also generally excluded except in respect of severance monies.

3.2.7 As stated hereinabove, the principal statute giving effect to statutory minimum terms and conditions of employment is the BCEA. The stated purpose of the Act is to advance economic development and social justice by establishing and enforcing minimum conditions of employment, be it on a national or sectoral basis.

It is sometimes necessary to read any applicable wage-regulating measure together with the BCEA to obtain a complete picture of an employee's minimum conditions of employment, such as sectoral determinations or collective bargaining agreements that might apply.

3.2.8 The BCEA uses the mechanism of basic employment standards and determination to fix minimum standards, which can then be made applicable nationally or by means of sectoral application. Section 4 of the Act (referred to above) provides that a basic condition of employment constitutes a term of a contract of employment, except to the extent that:

- any law provides for a more favourable term; or
- a term of the contract of employment is more favourable to the employee than the basic condition of employment.

3.2.9 Chapter 8 of the BCEA provides for the promulgation of important sectoral determinations which establishes basic ("customised") conditions of employment for certain sectors and areas, particularly where collective bargaining is absent. Sectoral determinations are promulgated for those sectors of the economy that are traditionally relatively unorganised or difficult to organise, for example domestic workers, farm workers, the retail sector and the security sector. A sectoral determination may set minimum rates of remuneration and other terms including hours of work, leave, minimum standards for housing and sanitation, and the like.

In respect of this chapter the Toolkit provides for the following information:

- BCEA Statutory Terms and Conditions.
- Schedule 8 of the LRA – A Code of Good Practice: Dismissal.
- LRA Schedule – A Code: Who is an Employee?
- Conventional Penalties Act.

CHAPTER 4

THE CONTRACT OF EMPLOYMENT: FORMATION, CONTENTS AND FORMAT

In this chapter, the importance of agreeing on clear and exact contractual duties and obligations, and the positive consequences for both employer and employee to have a written contract of employment that bonds the relationship between the parties, is examined.

"*It should be recalled though that a contract of employment may be in writing or oral, and its terms may be express or tacit. There are no formalities required for the formation of a contract of employment. Section 29 of the Basic Conditions of Employment Act 75 of 1997 requires 'written particulars of employment', to be given to an employee, it does not require a written contract. What is required therefore is a conspectus of all the relevant facts including any relevant contractual terms, and a determination whether these holistically viewed establish a relationship of employment as contemplated by the statutory definition*" (as per Van Niekerk J, in *Rumbles v Kwabat Marketing (Pty) Ltd* D1055/2001 [2003] ZALC 57).

4.1 Introduction

The contract of employment is defined as an agreement between an employer and employee, where the latter places services at the disposal and under the control of the employer in exchange for some form of remuneration.

The essential element of such a contract can be summarised as being:

- a voluntary agreement;
- individually between employer and employee;
- for work and services to be rendered;
- under the control and authority of the employer; and
- in exchange for some form of remuneration.

4.2 The Element of Control and 'The Right to Manage'

The element of control is a hallmark feature of the contract of employment and also provides for one of the distinctions between the latter and the contract of an independent contractor.

When an employment agreement is entered into the employer has the right to organise, lead, control and distribute the work of the employee. In modern employment relations characterised by increased specialisation and expertise, the employer may have very little control over the manner in which the employee performs tasks, and key employees in particular bear an increased amount of responsibility and accountability.

For actual control, it is not necessary for there to be micro-management control on a day-to-day basis. For the purposes of the employment contract, only the right to exercise control over the activities of the employee needs to be vested in the employer. The employer need not exercise the right at all and this will not mean that such right has been compromised, abrogated or, in fact, that it is absent.

The employer, however, does not have unfettered discretion and is not entirely at liberty to manage and control the work as it sees fit, and such right is limited by wide-ranging employment legislation as well as related protocols.

No matter the power, significance and extent of protective legislation, the contract of employment obligations, or the skills, qualifications and experience of the employee, in the final analysis employers still retain the ultimate leverage because of the right to decide on pay and remuneration, as well as to dismiss.

4.3 Validity Requirements

The general requirements in order to conclude a binding contract are applicable to employment contracts as well. These are as follows:

- There must be **consensus** on the key terms, i.e. the work to be performed, the applicable remuneration, and the duration of the contract.
- Each party must have the **capacity** to contract, and must be legally capable of performing agreed obligations.
- Each party must be **legally competent** to perform the rights and duties assumed.
- The rights and duties created must be **possible and permitted by law**.

4.4 **Formation and Formalities**

In terms of common law there are no formalities to be completed by the parties, and the contract comes into being upon the acceptance of the offer of employment, either expressly or tacitly.

Section 29 (Written Particulars of Employment) of the BCEA requires an employer to furnish "written particulars" of employment to employees, inclusive of the identity of the parties, work to be performed, rate of pay, conditions of employment, annual leave, sick leave entitlement, and so forth. Section 29 fulfils an administrative function and does not in itself constitute a contract of employment (though it can serve as evidence of some of the key terms of such contract). This section merely sets out the substantive, statutory basic conditions of employment and the rights to these conditions, for the benefit of the parties. Such BCEA schedule must be displayed on the employer's premises, normally in a poster format. (For a Written Particulars of Employment schedule see the Toolkit section.)

Although there is no requirement for the contract of employment or letter of appointment to be in writing, the same should be reduced to writing for the sake of clarity and good and responsible management, as well as to avoid energy sapping and costly disputes in respect of what the intentions of the parties were, or could have been.

An important issue is the manner and method of the employment offer made by the employer (the offerer) to the employee (the offeree). The offer and acceptance can, for instance, take place:

- at the employment interview;
- during a telephone conversation; or
- by exchange of letters.

In addition, the following four points must be noted:

- The acceptance of the offer of employment must be clear, unequivocal and unambiguous (either in writing, by e-mail, SMS, WhatsApp, orally or tacitly – with the latter possibly being problematic for obvious reasons).
- The acceptance of the offer must correspond with the contents of the offer.
- Acceptance of the offer must be made in accordance with the mode presented by the offerer.
- Acceptance of the offer must be communicated to the offerer verbally, electronically or by SMS/WhatsApp.

An employer may withdraw an offer of employment if the candidate has not yet accepted it, unless the offer has stated that it is open for a defined period in which case it cannot be withdrawn until that period expires. Once the offer has been accepted, whether verbally or in writing, the employer cannot withdraw it or unilaterally change any of the terms without risking an action of breach of contract.

Finally, let's rewind for a minute. Remember, all employees have contracts of employment, whether those have been concluded orally or in writing.

A written contract is undoubtedly the preferred manner of conducting the employment relationship. It is also the employer's chance to set out exactly what is expected from the employee, and to lay the foundation of a good relationship. In addition, it significantly reduces the possibility of unnecessary disputes and opportunism, for instance fabricating or conjuring up imaginary or non-existent rights in the future.

In any individual labour dispute, the first step will be to examine the contract of employment as the initial source of all duties and obligations. Such contract will provide for indispensable dispute-related information, ranging from a claim for damages to an age or 'pensionable' dismissal, or to determine the contractual status of the employer's disciplinary code.

4.5 **Duties and Obligations**

The employer's common law duties in terms of the contract of employment are fairly simple and straightforward. They consist of the duty to:

- provide work as agreed;
- pay the employee; and
- provide safe working conditions.

In addition, statute law, and in particular the provisions of the LRA, BCEA, EEA, Safety and Health legislation, and in the case of civil servants, the Public Service Act, provide for a raft of employer duties and obligations.

The employee's contractual obligations can be briefly stated as being to:

- provide work and maintain reasonable efficiency;
- obey and carry out reasonable instructions;
- act in good faith and in the best interests of the employer;
- be loyal and respectful; and
- refrain from misconduct generally.

The above-mentioned duties are normally added to or expanded upon with the following:

- Contract of employment terms and conditions.
- Addendums to contract.
- Standard Operating Procedures (SOPs).
- Rules of conduct and capacity.
- Changes in work methods and operational re-organisation.
- Communication and employee monitoring.
- Remuneration and incentive schemes.
- Employee benefits.
- Work performance improvement plans.
- Safety and health measures.
- Induction procedures and agreed or stated performance standards.

The contract of employment or appointment letter must be simple and concise - ideally a 'skeletal agreement' with condition of employment details, addendums, SOPs etc. contained separately in the employer's policy manual or Employee Handbook. The intention can never be to attempt to "cover all the bases", as this could be an exercise in futility.

A successful Employee Handbook cuts down on misunderstandings; its purpose is to communicate employer policies and procedures clearly and directly to employees. Such an Employee Handbook could include the following:

- The employer's mission statement.
- General conditions of employment.
- Absenteeism management.
- Salary and performance reviews.
- Communications inclusive of internet policies.
- Health and safety regulations.
- Leave regulations.
- Benefit schemes, e.g. Pension Fund, Provident Fund, Medical Aid.

(Samples of policies and procedures that should be included in an Employee Handbook are contained in the Toolkit section of this book.)

Employers must ensure they reach consensus regarding the exact duties of their employees as well as their Key Performance Areas (KPAs), inclusive of standards of performance and the achievement of targets. A separate agreement for attachment to the contract should be entered into for this purpose. (For a sample KPA Performance Agreement see the annexure provided in the Toolkit section.)

4.6 Contract Terms - Express, Implied, Statutory Rights and Others

4.6.1 Express terms

These are the terms that the employer and employee have specifically agreed to in writing or verbally, for instance the nature of the job and the duration thereof.

4.6.2 Tacit and implied terms: unwritten understandings

Unwritten understandings (i.e. tacit and implied terms of "custom and practice") are part and parcel of contracts of employment, without having been written into such contract, nor expressly provided for.

Unwritten understandings and implied terms come into existence with the passage of time, the custom and practice of the enterprise or economic sector, as well as the nature of the employer's business. Most verbal contracts of employment rely solely on the existence of such tacit and implied terms, which could range over a very wide spectrum of duties and obligations.

Yet a longstanding practice needs to be of sufficient importance and gravity to be contractually binding. The courts have ruled, for instance, that a regular barbecue held before the employer's annual shut-down could not constitute a tacit term, as the barbecue was conducted as be a "voluntary gesture of appreciation".

Importantly implied terms cannot override express terms, and to be implied by custom and practice, terms must be:

- certain;
- reasonable; and
- either well-established or known to the majority of the employees.

4.6.3 Statutory rights

As mentioned above, in terms of section 29 of the BCEA, employers must provide all employees with a written statement of particulars of employment consisting of basic statutory employment conditions. (A copy of such document is included in the Toolkit section of this book.) All employees are entitled to the statutory rights so provided for.

4.6.4 Penalty 'claw back' clauses

Some employers often use contractual 'claw back' provisions to protect their position where employees might renege on agreements. By way of example, an employment contract may provide that the employer can recoup the cost of training, placement or relocating an employee if the employment is terminated as a result of the employee's breach. Such a provision confirms the commercial nature of the contract and provides some cover for the employer in the event of possible abuse by the employee.

Some employers also resort to "retention bonuses", where key personnel are paid bonuses on condition that they will not terminate their employment within a specified time period.

Such a 'penalty clause' is a stipulation in a contract where the parties agree that if one of them does not comply with certain arrangements, requirements or instructions, a certain sum of money has to be paid. This can include a variety of issues such as desertion, breach of trade secrets and confidentiality, or premature resignation or non-completion of contract, to name but a few.

There is an increased tendency for 'penalty clauses' to be introduced in South Africa, primarily for financial and cost-saving measures, as well as to make errant employees responsible to their employers for financial losses suffered as a result of the actions of employees. The Conventional Penalties Act (CPA) of 1962 permits these clauses, but allows a court to reduce the amount claimed. In fact, a court is obliged to investigate the relationship between the penalty and the prejudice suffered, and establish whether the penalty is out of proportion to the damages suffered (which has to be proved by the person hit by the penalty). An example of this is an employee who receives a "retention bonus" for R500,000 on condition that he remains in the service of the employer for a period of five years. Four years and 10 months later he resigns. In terms of the provisions of the CPA, the employer is not entitled to the full amount of R500,000, and a scale will be applied to determine the amount the employer is entitled to, based on the shortfall of two months.

With regard to these 'claw back' clauses, employers must be clear as to what legitimate interest they are seeking to protect, and how the sum payable is in line with the loss likely to be suffered in the event of a breach. This will be construed as at the time the contract was entered into, not at the time of the breach. Ultimately, employers should continue to ensure that the purpose of such clauses is compensatory and to recoup real losses, rather than to act as a deterrent.

The validity of these clauses are regularly tested by our Courts. An important test is whether the parties intended for the recovery clause to operate in terrorem as a penalty, a fine, punishment or a deterrent. A clause in a contract of employment will not pass scrutiny if it was intended as a 'weapon in terrorem.' 'Intended terror' will include a stipulation to force an employee not to leave or to face an exorbitant pay-back amount, in order to be so 'tagged and released.'

The employer must be able to prove that he is recovering the monies for financial compensation and not for nefarious and/or ulterior motives.

(A copy of the CPA and a sample 'penalty clause' is included in the Toolkit section.)

4.6.5 **Force majeure**

"*Force majeure*" circumstances relate to so-called "Acts of God", and literally means a "superior force" over which parties have little or no control.

The intention of a *force majeure* clause, inclusive of the common law concept of "supervening impossibility", is for the failure of a party to perform its obligations to be discharged as a result of an event, and such failure becomes "excusable". This would have the effect of protecting that party from valid claims for breach of contract, which would normally allow the innocent party to claim damages and/or cancel the contract.

In employment relations, a *force majeure* clause usually provides that if a *force majeure* event is protracted, the parties should be required to meet and to attempt to negotiate and agree a mutually acceptable outcome, and possibly to agree on alternatives and/or feasible courses of action.

An example clause to this effect in contracts of employment, could read as follows:

> *"If either the employer or the employee is prevented from performing any obligations in terms of this contract as a result of any event beyond its control including a pandemic, wars, riots, earthquakes, hurricanes or continued terrorism, neither party shall be liable for any failure to perform its obligations while such event persists, and either party shall have the right to terminate the contract if the event persists for a period in excess of 30 days."*

The concept is legally technical as well as complicated, and is certainly not as simplistic as it might seem on the surface. The High Court in *Glencore Grain Africa (Pty) Ltd v Du Plessis NO & others* [2007] JOL 21043 (O) held that there are certain conditions that must be fulfilled in order for a *force majeure* to trigger the type of impossibility that extinguishes a party's contractual obligations. These have been summed up as follows:

- The impossibility must be objectively impossible.
- It must be absolute as proposed to probable.
- It must be absolute as opposed to relative (in other words if the impossibility relates to something that can in general be done, but the one party seeking to escape liability cannot personally perform, such party remains liable).
- The impossibility must be unavoidable by "a reasonable person".
- Either party must not be at fault.
- The fact that a disaster or event was foreseeable does not necessarily mean that it ought to have been foreseeable, or that it is avoidable by a reasonable person.

4.6.6 Discretionary terms and restraint of trade

"Discretionary terms", e.g. the option to pay an annual discretionary bonus, could be included in the contract. Such a term should be exercised on a genuinely discretionary basis rather than on a consistent or guaranteed basis. Where the discretionary term is exercised in the employee's favour on a consistent basis, this may eventually have the effect of converting it into a contractual entitlement.

Restraint of trade, and sometimes "confidentiality" clauses, especially in respect of key employees, also could be a term of the contract. These are clauses inserted to restrict what an employee may do following termination of employment, and typically will include reference to a geographic area and a specified time period. Restraint of trade clauses and agreements are only reluctantly enforced by the courts because they are essentially viewed as an impediment on individuals from earning a living, and therefore not in the public interest. In exceptional cases, however, where the employer can clearly prove prejudice and irretrievable harm to the business, an employee will be contractually restrained.

Restraint clauses typically seek to prevent employees after termination of employment from:

- moving to work for a competitor;
- setting up in competition with the employer;
- seeking to persuade the employer's clients to do business with them in their new employment; and/or
- poaching the employer's staff.

(A guideline note on Restraint of Trade appears in the Toolkit section of the book.)

4.7 **Changes, Variations and Amendments to the Contract, and Contract Administration**

Changes or variations of the terms of a contract cannot be unilaterally resorted to by a party. Normally, the employer would wish to update and amend contracts of employment in order to introduce new work requirements and changed conditions of employment, for instance reductions in salary.

The contract of employment need not be physically amended and/or updated as a result of changed circumstances or other necessary amendments that may become relevant with the fullness of time, for instance improved salary packages, changed reporting relationships, and statutory consent in respect of medical testing and/or medical treatment.

With regard to contract maintenance and administration, the most productive course of action is for the employer to advise employees in writing of any new conditions and to confirm the same by email and/or by issuing written standard operating procedures, and as necessary, to consult with employees. Documentation related to the amendments, changes and variations can be filed with, or separately from, the original contract of employment document. The agreement of an employee should be obtained prior to the introduction of the change and a valid reason for such change must exist.

Should the employee refuse to agree to the change or changes, the continued tendering of services could provide evidence of condonation for such change, implied agreement, and/or consent, unless the employee lodged an objection at the time of the change.

Some operational and collective policy changes, for instance amendments to benefit schemes, provident or pension funds and medical aid scheme adjustments, are not subject to the general prohibition and can be introduced without individual consent.

It is not advisable to have an open-ended (read flexible) 'catch-all' variation clause where the employee purportedly gives consent to all future amendments and changes to the contract. At the time the parties will still need to agree to the new term or condition, in accordance with the principles of contract law. It is, however, possible to stipulate in the contract that certain conditions may be amended without consent, for instance discretionary bonuses, the shift system, and the most efficient production and work methods.

The disgruntled employee can allege breach of contract in response to the unilateral change and/or is entitled to the dispute resolution mechanisms of section 64(4) or 186 of the LRA.

4.8 Interpretation of Contracts

Generally, the following basic principles are followed when it becomes necessary to interpret the terms and conditions of contracts:

4.8.1 Determining mutual intentions

The first step is to determine the intentions shared by both parties. Courts and arbitrators will always first attempt to interpret a contract according to what the contract's authors originally intended. When possible, the mutual intentions will be determined strictly by using the written provisions included in the contract. If the contract's language is clear and definable, the contract language will control the interpretation. If the contract's language is unclear, if not vague, external evidence may be used to interpret intent. An example of this would be evidence of previous, similar situations and practices between the employer and the employee.

4.8.2 Ordinary meaning

In order to determine if the contract's language is clear and definite, there will be general reliance on the ordinary meaning of the word or phrase in question.

This practice is also known as going by the "dictionary definition" of the word, or literal meaning thereof. A contract will typically be interpreted by using ordinary means, unless it is clear that the drafter of the contract used the term in question in a technical or special way. An example of this would be how in a construction setting the word hammer could refer to a specific tool, whereas in other circumstances it may refer to a part of a gun.

4.8.3 **Some other aspects of contract interpretation include, but are not limited to:**

- **As a whole:** Contracts are generally interpreted as a whole, meaning that the definition of one word or term in one part of the contract should apply to the rest of the contract, unless otherwise specified; and
- **External evidence:** In general, the contract in itself will be used when interpreting the disputed term. However, if the particular terms of the contract in question are vague or ambiguous, the court may in exceptional circumstances decide to disregard the contract and instead use an external document to interpret the contract.

4.8.4 The principles for the interpretation of contracts were summarised by the SCA in *Natal Joint Municipal Pension Fund v Emdumeni Municipality* (2012 (4) SA 593 (SCA) para [18]), as follows:

> *"Over the last century there have been significant developments in the law relating to the interpretation of documents, both in this country and in others that follow similar rules to our own. It is unnecessary to add unduly to the burden of annotations by crawling through the case law on the construction of documents in order to trace those developments. The relevant authorities are collected and summarised in Bastian Financial Services (Pty) Ltd v General Hendrik Schoeman Primary School. The present state of the law can be expressed as follows. Interpretation is the process of attributing meaning to the words used in a document, be it legislation, some other statutory instrument, or contract, having regard to the context provided by reading the particular provision or provisions in the light of the document as a whole and the circumstances attendant upon its coming into existence. Whatever the nature of the document, consideration must be given to the language used in the light of the ordinary rules of grammar and syntax; the context in which the provision appears; the apparent purpose to which it is directed and the material known to those responsible for its production. Where more than one meaning is possible each possibility must be weighed in the light of all these factors. The process is objective not subjective. A sensible meaning is to be preferred to one that leads to insensible or unbusinesslike results*

or undermines the apparent purpose of the document. Judges must be alert to, and guard against, the temptation to substitute what they regard as reasonable, sensible or businesslike for the words actually used. To do so in regard to a statute or statutory instrument is to cross the divide between interpretation and legislation. In a contractual context it is to make a contract for the parties other than the one they in fact made. The 'inevitable point of departure is the language of the provision itself', read in context and having regard to the purpose of the provision and the background to the preparation and production of the document."

4.8.5 Finally, in respect of the rules pertaining to the interpretation of contracts, it must be borne in mind that the clause concerned will be construed on the basis of its construction at the time of the conclusion of the contract, and not at the time of any breach.

4.9 **Types of Contracts**

Contracts of employment basically consist of two types, both of which are related to contract duration, i.e.:

- permanent (indefinite); and
- temporary (fixed-term).

As discussed above, there are various forms and permutations as a result of an employer's business operations and the time that will be needed to complete work undertaken, be it as a project, phase or seasonal requirement.

In respect of permanent contracts, the intentions of the parties are that the contract will continue until the death of the employee or when retirement age is reached.

Temporary contracts of employment are subject to a specific period by stipulating a termination date, or by stipulating that the contract will terminate upon the occurrence of a particular future event, e.g. the completion of a bridge, the completion of phase two of the mine shaft, or the end of the harvest, or the termination of the employer's contract by the client of the employer.

The courts and the authorities have taken a critical, if not sceptical, view of temporary or fixed-term contracts of employment in general, as a result of some abuse and opportunistic implementation of contract terms in order to prejudice employees, to circumvent labour laws, and to unfairly dismiss temporary employees.

The provisions of section 198B of the LRA has drastically curtailed the use of temporary contracts for most employees, as an employer may not employ a person on a fixed-term contract of employment for more than a period of three months (unless certain exceptions apply). The on the face of it draconian provisions of section 198 B, are not as restrictive as might seem to be the case and in particular sub-sections 2, 3 and 4 provides for ample temporary employment possibilities. This section is repeated herein as follows:

"198B Fixed-term contracts with employees earning below earnings threshold

(1) For the purpose of this section, a "fixed-term contract" means a contract of employment that terminates on-

(a) the occurrence of a specified event;

(b) the completion of a specified task or project; or

(c) a fixed date, other than an employee's normal or agreed retirement age, subject to subsection (3).

(2) This section does not apply to-

(a) employees earning in excess of the threshold prescribed by the Minister in terms of section 6(3) of the Basic Conditions of Employment Act.

(b) an employer that employs less than 10 employees, or that employs less than 50 employees and whose business has been in operation for less than two years, unless-

(i) the employer conducts more than one business; or

(ii) the business was formed by the division or dissolution for any reason of an existing business; and

(c) an employee employed in terms of a fixed-term contract which is permitted by any statute, sectoral determination or collective agreement.

(3) An employer may employ an employee on a fixed-term contract or successive fixed-term contracts for longer than three months of employment only if-

(a) the nature of the work for which the employee is employed is of a limited or definite duration; or

(b) the employer can demonstrate any other justifiable reason for fixing the term of the contract.

(4) Without limiting the generality of subsection (3), the conclusion of a fixed-term contract will be justified if the employee-

(a) *is replacing another employee who is temporarily absent from work;*

(b) *is employed on account of a temporary increase in the volume of work which is not expected to endure beyond 12 months;*

(c) *is a student or recent graduate who is employed for the purpose of being trained or gaining work experience in order to enter a job or profession;*

(d) *is employed to work exclusively on a specific project that has a limited or defined duration;*

(e) *is a non-citizen who has been granted a work permit for a defined period;*

(f) *is employed to perform seasonal work;*

(g) *is employed for the purpose of an official public works scheme or similar public job creation scheme;*

(h) *is employed in a position which is funded by an external source for a limited period; or*

(i) *has reached the normal or agreed retirement age applicable in the employer's business.*

(5) *Employment in terms of a fixed-term contract concluded or renewed in contravention of subsection (3) is deemed to be of indefinite duration.*

(6) *An offer to employ an employee on a fixed-term contract or to renew or extend a fixed-term contract, must-*

(a) *be in writing; and*

(b) *state the reasons contemplated in subsection (3) (a) or (b).*

(7) *If it is relevant in any proceedings, an employer must prove that there was a justifiable reason for fixing the term of the contract as contemplated in subsection (3) and that the term was agreed.*

(8) (a) *An employee employed in terms of a fixed-term contract for longer than three months must not be treated less favourably than an employee employed on a permanent basis performing the same or similar work, unless there is a justifiable reason for different treatment.*

(b) *Paragraph (a) applies, three months after the commencement of the Labour Relations Amendment Act 2014, to fixed-term contracts of employment entered into before the commencement of the Labour Relations Amendment Act, 2014.*

(9) *As from the commencement of the Labour Relations Amendment Act, 2014 an employer must provide an employee employed in terms of a fixed-term contract and an employee employed on a permanent basis with equal access to opportunities to apply for vacancies*

(10) (a) An employer who employs an employee in terms of a fixed-term contract for a reason contemplated in subsection (4) (d) for a period exceeding 24 months must, subject to the terms of any applicable collective agreement, pay the employee on expiry of the contract one week's remuneration for each completed year of the contract calculated in accordance with section 35 of the Basic Conditions of Employment Act.

(b) An employee employed in terms of a fixed-term contract, as contemplated in paragraph (a), before the commencement of the Labour Relations Amendment Act, 2014, is entitled to the remuneration contemplated in paragraph (a) in respect of any period worked after the commencement of the said Act.

(11) An employee is not entitled to payment in terms of subsection (10) if, prior to the expiry of the fixed-term contract, the employer offers the employee employment or procures employment for the employee with a different employer, which commences at the expiry of the contract and on the same or similar terms.

198C Part-time employment of employees earning below earnings threshold

(1) For the purpose of this section-

(a) a part-time employee is an employee who is remunerated wholly or partly by reference to the time that the employee works and who works less hours than a comparable full-time employee; and

(b) a comparable full-time employee-

(i) is an employee who is remunerated wholly or partly by reference to the time that thc employee works and who is identifiable as a full-time employee in terms of the custom and practice of the employer of that employee; and

(ii) does not include a full time employee whose hours of work are temporarily reduced or operational requirement as a result of an agreement.

(2) This section does not apply-

(a) to employees earning in excess of the threshold determined by the Minister in terms of section 6(3) of the Basic Conditions of Employment Act;

(b) to an employer that employs less than 10 employees or that employs less than 50 employees and whose business has been in operation for less than two years unless-

(i) *the employer conducts more than one business; or*

(ii) *the business was formed by the division or dissolution, for any reason, of an existing business;*

(c) *to an employee who ordinarily works less than 24 hours a month for an employer; and*

(d) *during an employee's first three months of continuous employment with an employer.*

(3) *Taking into account the working hours of a part-time employee, irrespective of when the part-time employee was employed, an employee must-*

(a) *treat a part-time employee on the whole not less favourably than a comparable full-time employee doing the same or similar work, unless there is a justifiable reason for different treatment; and*

(b) *provide a part-time employee with access to training and skills development on the whole not less favourable than the access applicable to a comparable full-time employee."*

4.10 **Contents of Contracts of Employment**

The general, unfounded belief that a detailed, voluminous letter of appointment (or contract) will be a panacea in anticipation of future problems can result in an over-regulated contract which serves little purpose, and in fact could be indicative of mistrust from the employer's side.

As stated above, the idea can never be to reduce all aspects of the relationship to writing.

A simple, basic "skeletal" contract will consist of the following:

1. Particulars of the parties.
2. The nature of the job and key performance areas.
3. Implied warranty of suitability to perform.
4. Duration.
5. Remuneration.
6. Substantive conditions of employment and employee benefits.
7. Safety and health.

8. Standard rules and regulations, policies and procedures and standard operating procedures.
9. Legal formalities.
10. Termination of contract.

Items 1 to 5, as well as items 9 to 10, will ideally be contained in the contract or letter of appointment. Items 6, 7 and 8 will normally be incorporated into the contract of employment by means of appendices or in the employer's separate policies and procedures referred to as the Employment Handbook.

Disciplinary Codes and Procedures, Grievance Procedures and Rules of Conduct should not be included in the contract *per se*, and must be considered to be employment guidelines other than contractual terms and undertakings. For all practical purposes and intent, the LRA's Code of Good Practice - Dismissal, supersedes internal disciplinary and incapacity procedures. It is still advisable, however, for the employer to have a customised, internal disciplinary code, listing and treating transgressions in order of severity in order to establish the employer's disciplinary "culture" and policy. (See appendices in the Toolkit section for sample disciplinary codes.)

4.11 **The Code of Good Practice: Dismissal**

This statutory "guideline" Code requires that fairness (for purposes of section 188(1) of the LRA), must be interpreted in the light of the contents of the Code. The provisions of the Code consist of a set of guidelines rather than rules - which are in its own words "intentionally general" - which must be taken into consideration when assessing whether a dismissal is fair s(188(2)). The effect is to create a presumption that the Code should be followed rather than there being a duty to do so. Action in manifest conflict with the provisions of the Code might, in the absence of good cause, be regarded as a failure to take the Code into account, and could conceivably be remedied by an order of the Labour Court requiring statutory compliance.

It follows that the Code cannot be given an interpretation that is in conflict with the LRA and in the event of such conflict the LRA must prevail. Nor can the Code supersede dismissal provisions contained in individual contracts of employment, or dismissal procedures that are contained in collective bargaining agreements. Only where such agreed procedures are silent, or in the event of incorporation of the Code, will it apply.

Increasingly employers are using the Code, correctly so, as a substitute for having internal disciplinary, ill-health and poor performance procedures.

4.12 Statutory Terms and Conditions of Employment: Automatic Contractual Inclusion

The BCEA, by means of section 4, regulates contracts of employment and provides for minimum terms and conditions of employment. No contract of employment may provide for less favourable terms than such prescribed conditions. Section 29 (Written Particulars of Employment) provides that the employer must supply the employee with such particulars, which are contained in the Toolkit section of the book. These minimum terms and conditions include, but are not limited to, the below:

- **Work Hours**: an employee may not work more than 45 hours a week or more than eight hours (if a week is six days long) or nine hours a day (if a week is five days long).
- **Overtime**: (by agreement) an employee may not work more than 10 hours' overtime per week and the agreed upon overtime may also not cause the employee to work more than 12 hours per day. An employer must pay an employee 1.5 times his/her daily wage for overtime worked or give him/her time off instead of payment. An employee who usually does not work on a Saturday is entitled to twice his/her daily wage.
- **Lunch**: an employee must be given 60-minute break after five continuous hours of work, however this may be reduced to a 30-minute break by agreement or be cancelled if an employee works less than six hours a day.
- **Annual Leave**:
    - Annual - 21 continuous days of leave on full pay or by agreement, one day's leave on full pay for every 17 days of work during a 12-month period, or one hour's leave for every 17 hours of work. Leave must be taken during or within six months after the 12-month period has ended.
- **Maternity Leave**: four continuous months' leave without pay. (Benefits from the Unemployment Insurance Fund are available and the mother can return to work after six weeks of giving birth, unless the earlier return is certified by a medical practitioner or midwife).
- **Parental Leave**: 10 consecutive days of leave without pay. (Benefits from the Unemployment Insurance Fund are available to the parent of a child who does not qualify for any other type of leave, for example, a father of a child).
- **Adoption Leave**: an adoptive parent of a child below the age of two is entitled to at least 10 consecutive weeks of leave without pay. (Benefits from the Unemployment Insurance Fund are available. If there are two adoptive parents,

it is possible for one to apply for adoption leave and the other can apply for parental leave.)

- **Commissioning Parental Leave**: a commissioning parent (a parent to a child born through surrogacy) is entitled to at least 10 consecutive weeks of leave without pay. (Benefits from the Unemployment Insurance Fund are available. If there are two commissioning parents, one can apply for commissioning parental leave and the other can apply for parental leave.)
- **Family Leave**: after the first four months of employment, three days' leave on full pay during a 12-month period (an employee must work more than four days a week). Proof of birth, illness or death of a child, or death of a spouse, life partner, parent, grandparent, grandchild or sibling, may be required.
- **Remuneration**: daily, weekly or monthly payment of compensation in Rands (can be in cash or by electronic transfer into an employee's bank account) and/or in kind (undefined) by no later than seven days after it becomes due. A pay slip must be provided showing the calculation of remuneration and all deductions made, if any.
- **Termination of Employment**: a minimum notice period must be given when employment is terminated by either party, as follows:
    - One week's notice, if employed for less than six months.
    - Two weeks' notice, if employed for more than six months but less than one year.
    - Four weeks' notice, if employed for more than one year.
    - Payment of notice instead of the employee working his/her notice period.

On termination, an employer must pay an employee any outstanding compensation, overtime, annual leave, etc. An employee must be given a certificate of service, but there is no obligation to provide a testimony. Written particulars of employment must be provided with termination of employment. Some of the above terms and conditions do not apply to employees earning an income above a certain statutory amount ('threshold'), those working less than 24 hours a month, those on continuous shift, or in the case of employees regulating their own hours of work.

- **Contract of Employment Clauses**

Sample contract clauses are available in the contracts and letter of appointment example provided in the Toolkit section. The following clauses are listed as clauses that are traditionally in employment relations, which are considered to be contentious. Whereas employees will readily agree, accept and sign for the clauses upon commencement of employment, it often becomes extremely difficult to obtain employee consent and/or agreement in respect of the following once employment has commenced:

- Deductions from salary
- Discretionary reductions in pay
- Medical testing
- Sick leave penalties
- Unauthorised absenteeism
- *Force majeure*
- Medical examination
- Polygraph and alcohol testing, and searching consent
- Financial penalty "claw back"
- Variation, changes and amendments
- Age and retirement policy
- Restraint of trade and confidentiality
- Vaccination consent
- Performance targets
- Privacy and electronic surveillance

For the purposes of this chapter, most, if not all, of the contents of the Toolkit will be of relevance, inclusive of all the contracts, policies and procedures provided for, as well as the BCEA Statutory Minimum Conditions of Employment.

NOTE: Further and/or additional sample contracts of employment material, inclusive of applicable clauses, are provided for in Chapter 6 of this book which deals with WFH contracts.

CHAPTER 5

TERMINATION OF EMPLOYMENT

"It lasted for a long time, I believe. A very long time. It was a great success, but even great successes come to a natural end." (Isaac Asimov, *Robots and Empire - Robot, #4*)

In this chapter, the basics of the termination of contracts of employment are reviewed, with some pointers provided, especially in respect of what could be tricky situations such as resignation and age and retirement dismissals.

5.1 Introduction

In accordance with the principles of Contract Law, the termination of a contract of employment is a relatively simple process.

No reason need be given in the case of a termination on notice in accordance with ordinary common law principles, as the common law does not concern itself with the reason for the termination of employment. As long as the contractual or statutory provisions relating to the notice have been complied with, the requirements of the common law are satisfied and the termination is regarded as being lawful. Whether the dismissal is fair or not is a separate issue.

The concept of fairness of a dismissal has its origin in the LRA. In terms of the provisions of the LRA, a dismissal must be fair, which means that the dismissal must comply with certain substantive and procedural requirements. Even though a dismissal is lawful (in compliance with the law and contract itself), this does not mean that it will necessarily be fair.

It is therefore important to distinguish between a 'lawful' termination of an employment contract and a 'fair' termination of the contract. In essence, a lawful termination means either that the terms and conditions of the contract relating to the giving of notice have been complied with, or that the contract was summarily terminated on the grounds of a fundamental malperformance of a duty.

If either party summarily terminates the contract of employment on the grounds of breach of contract, the breach of contract must indeed have been of a serious nature. If the breach is not serious enough to justify termination, the subsequent termination will be unlawful.

If all the contractual requirements for giving notice have been complied with, that termination is lawful because it is in accordance with the contract. If the period of notice has not been complied with, and no payment in lieu of notice has been given, that notice of termination will be unlawful, as it will be a breach of contract.

5.2 **Fairness**

The LRA "duty of fairness" does not mean that employment contractual provisions are subordinate.

> *"If the constitutional dispensation did have the effect of introducing into the employment relationship a reciprocal duty it does not follow that it deprives contractual terms of their effect. Such implied duties would operate to ameliorate the effect of unfair terms in the contract, or even to supplement the contractual terms where necessary, but not to deprive a fair contract of its legal effect. The procedure provided for in the disciplinary code was clearly a fair one - it would hardly be open to the appellant (the employer) to suggest that it was not - and the respondent (the employee) was entitled to insist that the appellant abide by its undertaking to apply it. It is no answer to say that the alternative procedure adopted by the appellant was just as good." - Denel (Pty) Ltd v Vorster* (2004) 25 ILJ 659 (SCA).

Fair contractual terms and conditions, as agreed to by the employer and the employee, will therefore retain their legal force and effect, and can be enforced by the employee if the employer breached a contractual term, and *vice versa.* Section 23(1) of the Constitution introduced an implied duty on both the employer and the employee to act fairly.

5.3 **Instances of Termination**

Contracts of employment may be terminated by:

- the giving of notice by either party;
- Resignation;
- the effluxion of time;
- completion of contract period;

- for any cause recognised by law (termination on the basis of misconduct, incapacity or operational requirements);
- by operation of law;
- the death of the employee;
- the insolvency of the employer;
- by mutual agreement;
- the death of the employer;
- repudiation and breach of contract; and/or
- statutory unfair dismissals.

The contract can also come to an end by agreement, in an amicable and decorous manner. For instance, the employee gives notice for reasons of a career advancement opportunity, or when the employee retires.

More often than not, however, such termination of contract can provide for a stressful dynamic, as well as extremely unpleasant experience, as each party jockeys for position in order to defend the stance it has taken, with wild allegations and sometimes insults thrown around with gay abandon.

It is not the intention, for the purposes of this book, to provide for a detailed exposé on all of the instances of termination possibilities referred to hereinabove, thus only more pertinent aspects will be dealt with.

5.4 **Statutory Notice Periods**

As stated earlier in this book, sections 37 and 38 of the BCEA provide for the following notice periods, the contents of which are self-explanatory:

"37 Notice of termination of employment

(1) Subject to section 38, a contract of employment terminable at the instance of a party to the contract may be terminated only on notice of not less than-

(a) one week if the employee has been employed for six months or less;

(b) two weeks, if the employee has been employed for more than six months but not more than one year;

(c) four weeks, if the employee-

(i) has been employed for one year or more; or

(ii) is a farm worker or domestic worker who has been employed for more than six months.

(2) (a) A collective agreement may not permit a notice period shorter than that required by subsection (1).

(b) Despite paragraph (a), a collective agreement may permit the notice period of four weeks required by subsection (1) (c) (i) to be reduced to not less than two weeks.

(3) No agreement may require or permit an employee to give a period of notice longer than that required of the employer.

(4) (a) Notice of termination of a contract of employment must be given in writing, except when it is given by an illiterate employee.

(b) If an employee who receives a notice of termination is not able to understand it, the notice must be explained orally by, or on behalf of, the employer to the employee in an official language the employee reasonably understands.

(5) Notice of termination of a contract of employment given by an employer must-

(a) not be given during any period of leave to which the employee is entitled in terms of Chapter Three; and

(b) not run concurrently with any period of leave to which the employee is entitled in terms of Chapter Three, except sick leave.

(6) Nothing in this section affects the right-

(a) of a dismissed employee to dispute the lawfulness or fairness of the dismissal in terms of Chapter VIII of the Labour Relations Act, 1995, or any other law; and

(b) of an employer or an employee to terminate a contract of employment without notice for any cause recognised by law.

38 Payment instead of notice

(1) Instead of giving an employee notice in terms of section 37, an employer may pay the employee the remuneration of the employee would have received, calculated in accordance with section 35, if the employee had worked during the notice period.

(2) If an employee gives notice of termination of employment, and the employer waives any part of the notice, the employer must pay the remuneration referred to in subsection (1), unless the employer and the employee agree otherwise."

The notice periods prescribed hereinabove is included in contracts of employment. Although parties can agree to a longer period of notice, a shorter period can be agreed to.

5.5 **Resignation**

The act of resignation is a unilateral act by an employee, and does not need the employer's acceptance nor "blessing".

Unless agreed to the contrary, the employee must work out their notice period, but the employer has the discretion to pay the employee in lieu of notice. Should the employee refuse to work out the period of notice, the employer is not obliged to pay for the remainder of the notice period.

An employer is prohibited from giving notice and/or terminating the contract during any period of leave the employee is entitled to, except in the case of sick leave.

Notice periods also mean that the employer cannot require nor allow an employee to take annual leave during such time.

Often employees resign "with immediate effect" whilst on disciplinary suspension or to escape dismissal, or as a result of some other unpleasantness. Such action by the employee does not mean that the contract of employment has ceased to exist there and then as a result. The employer's right to discipline an employee during the notice period is retained irrespective of whether the resignation was "with immediate effect" or not, and the contract of employment only terminates at the end of the notice period.

In the important case of *Standard Bank of SA Ltd v Nombulelo Cynthia Chiloane* (JA 85/18 [2020]), legal certainty was created by the Labour Appeal Court confirming an employer's rights in respect of employees during a contractual or statutory notice period. The effect of the judgment is that an employee's failure to comply with notice period obligations amounts to repudiation. The employer can elect to either: (a) waive the notice period and terminate the contract; or (b) reject the repudiation and hold the employee to the notice period, inclusive of disciplining the employee during such notice period, or to require the employee to complete unfinished tasks, in accordance with the remedy of specific performance.

5.6 Causes Recognised by Law, for Termination of Employment and Dismissal

A contract of employment can be terminated at any stage for any reason or cause recognised in law as sufficient, i.e.:

- misconduct;
- incapacity; and
- operational requirements

A dismissal is in response to an act, omission or circumstances which entitle the employer to terminate the contract of employment in common law, or as contemplated by section 186(1) of the LRA, as well as the Code of Good Practice - Dismissal.

The ambit of this book does not extend to statutory unfair dismissal procedures and provisions, inclusive of the tenets of substance and procedural fairness. However, it is considered to be prudent to repeat section 186(1) and (2) of the LRA as follows:

"186 Meaning of dismissal and unfair labour practice

(1) ***'Dismissal'*** *means that-*

(a) *an employer has terminated employment with or without notice;*

(b) *an employee employed in terms of a fixed-term contract of employment reasonably expected the employer-*

(i) *to renew a fixed-term contract of employment on the same or similar terms but the employer offered to renew it on less favourable terms, or did not renew it; or*

(ii) *to retain the employee in employment on an indefinite basis but otherwise on the same or similar terms as the fixed-term contract, but the employer offered to retain the employee on less favourable terms, or did not offer to retain the employee;*

(c) *an employer refused to allow an employee to resume work after she-*

(i) *took maternity leave in terms of any law, collective agreement or her contract of employment;*

(d) *an employer who dismissed a number of employees for the same or similar reasons has offered to re-employ one or more of them but has refused to re-employ another; or*

(e) *an employee terminated employment with or without notice because the employer made continued employment intolerable for the employee; or*

(f) *an employee terminated employment with or without notice because the new employer, after a transfer in terms of section 197 or section 197A, provided the employee with conditions or circumstances at work that are substantially less favourable to the employee than those provided by the old employer.*

(2) ***'Unfair labour practice'*** *means any unfair at or omission that arises between an employer and an employee involving-*

(a) *unfair conduct by the employer relating to the promotion, demotion, probation (excluding disputes about dismissals for a reason relating to probation) or training of an employee or relating to the provision of benefits to an employee;*

(b) *the unfair suspension of an employee or any other unfair disciplinary action short of dismissal in respect of an employee;*

(c) *a failure or refusal by an employer to reinstate or re-employ a former employee in terms of any agreement; and*

(d) *an occupational detriment, other than dismissal, in contravention of the Protected Disclosures Act, 200 (Act 26 of 2000), on account of the employee having made a protected disclosure defined in that Act."*

The Toolkit section contains the following important information for the purposes of this chapter:

- KPAs and Performance Agreement
- Disciplinary Transgressions, Misconduct Code
- Absenteeism Policy and Procedure
- Poor Work Performance Policy and Procedure
- Medical Incapacity Policy and Procedure
- Retirement Policy and Procedure

CHAPTER 6

PUSHING THE FRONTIERS OF TRADITIONAL EMPLOYMENT - WORKING FROM HOME (WFH) AND HYBRID WORKING

Changes in society as a result of sometimes unpredictable external forces and developments will invariably impact on "bread and butter" issues and making a living. In this chapter, more flexible, hybrid and decentralised working is discussed, which has a profound effect on the nature and extent of the traditional core component of the contract of employment, i.e. the employer's control and authority over the employee.

6.1 **Introduction**

WFH in itself can be considered to be a vast subject, thus, for the purposes of this book, only a brief overview is provided of WFH (decentralised, remote or hybrid working), as well as its effects on, and consequences for, contracts of employment. With increased hybrid and remote working and decentralised exercise of control and authority, the contract of employment will become even more important as the source of all the rights, duties and arrangements between the parties.

Dependent on the needs, business and employment structure of the employer, WFH can also be classified as "atypical work", dealt with in Chapter 2 of this book. A WFH employment relationship does not always conform to the standard or typical static model of regular work performed under the direct control and supervision of the employer. In respect of WFH, the following points need mentioning:

6.1.1 Flexible working and hence the WFH concept is of course not a new way for businesses to operate and was prevalent previously - especially with smaller employers in predominantly white collar employment environments, where sales staff, for instance, had to be out of the office and would sometimes only clock in once a month.

6.1.2 The 2020 universal pandemic life-changing circumstances have compelled employers to take vast strides in deploying and managing flexible and remote workforces, and above all to maintain or to improve their productivity. Working arrangements reflect these differences and changes, and the efficient re-organisation of staff plays a key role in an organisation's survival.

6.1.3 Future employment will consist of a blended solution which allows for more flexibility all round – for employers to decide on who will work where, and for some employees to adapt to a new work environment and changed employment contractual terms and conditions.

With a segment of employees, especially those in support, marketing and sales functions having had to break away from the conventional office environment, some direct management control and authority had to be compromised, and the element of trust in the employment relationship has become far more pronounced, especially as it relates to employers' dependency on employees.

6.1.4 The migration of some employees to WFH is probably long overdue, and the pandemic has acted as a catalyst to finally put the wheels in motion in respect of this new way to work, and for employers to become more dependent on remote working employees, without direct control and supervision.

6.1.5 A properly planned and implemented remote working strategy is not only a necessity to survive and thrive in the digital-first world – it also provides for an opportunity to improve upon, if not to multiply, an organisation's impact and its market share. Company culture will continue to be a major determinant of successful employers and a people-centric emphasis will continue to serve employers well.

The famous quote, "culture eats strategy for breakfast", attributed to management consultant Peter Drucker, could not ring more true given the challenges brought on by drastic pandemic interventions.

6.1.6 A collaborative management style, which is inclusive of agility, adaptability and an increased reliance on trust and confidence in employees, is the essential and all important norm. It has also been recognised that remote and hybrid working can strengthen and diversify an organisation's talent pool, while simultaneously improving employee engagement by arguably providing them with a better work-life balance.

6.1.7 Any WFH model must, by necessity, take cognisance of the socio-economic and political environment and the challenges faced by some employees working from townships and unconventional suburbs. Unique circumstances to WFH office space, interferences with productivity, safety and security are some of the issues that will oblige employers to align work plans with the assistance of some reality checking.

6.2 The Hybrid WFH Model

6.2.1 A hybrid WFH model allows some employees to work remotely whilst others work on-site.

Within this structure, some teams or departments are split between working remotely and working at company premises. The marketing team may be off-site for example, while the sales crew reports at the office every morning. Certain positions or leadership roles may also be designated as fully-remote or in-company across all departments.

6.2.2 Employees who are allocated to WFH will spend most workdays remote (with the potential for occasional office visits). On-premises teams will do just the opposite. Creative as well as structural thinking thus needs to go into a WFH model.

First, policies and contractual arrangements must be revisited, and if necessary created and introduced, to benefit both WFH employees and on-site team members alike, even if they are slightly different. Care must be taken to treat employees equally to avoid the impression that there is preferential treatment; this sometimes happens in the case of remote teams with problematic consequences.

A positive work environment needs to exist and must be nurtured, where employees feel appreciated no matter where they clock-in.

6.2.3 In particular, the following aspects need to be attended to:

- Issue addendums or Standing Operating Procedures (SOPs) to contracts of employment in respect of a changed work format and procedural adjustments.
- Rewrite employees' KPAs as necessary and the specific tasks performed.
- Have regard to the individual employee, and consider that some personalities lend to working more readily WFH, and others less so.

- Introduce new reporting and communication structures to enhance flexibility and productivity.
- Introduce physical and mental well-being programmes.
- Overview personalised remuneration and team reward schemes; get expert advice and enter into separate employee agreements (addendums to contracts of employment).
- Review and monitor co-working tools: messaging, video conferencing and enhanced internet connectivity.
- Review employee monitoring and task attendance, scheduled meetings and tracking (legal compliance and consent requirements).
- Revise measures in respect of decentralised management, i.e. indirect, leading, organising and controlling.
- Monitor performance management, misconduct and ill-health processes and procedures, inclusive of social at home WFH conditions.

6.3 **Trust and Transparency**

6.3.1 Modern business practices and the resultant consequences on employment relations have pushed back the way in which the contract of employment's core component, i.e. control and authority, is exercised. Variations and permutations of the right to manage and control have developed; it is a question of degree, rather than a hard and fast rule, and "control" has to some extent given way to trust. As a result, people are learning how to do work disparately and with far less oversight: they are learning "on the job" what works and what doesn't work at home, which might have happened before, but never to such an extent.

6.3.2 Trust and confidence in the abilities of employees is the super ingredient to a productive distributive workforce, but beyond this, there are several other key strategies to make remote work a success. This includes how to prioritise and when to communicate with teams, and how to organise while making sure that everyone has the means to work on their priorities.

Central to this is setting clear expectations and then trusting employees to manage their own schedules, while not forgetting check-ins to ensure things stay on track.

6.4 The WFH Contract of Employment

6.4.1 The ramifications for individual contracts of employment have increased significantly, with employers having to rely more heavily on skilled, if not exceptional, employees, as well as the contractual, reciprocal arrangements entered into in order to get the job done and to keep the business competitive as well as profitable.

6.4.2 It is important for employers to note that there should be no separate contracts of employment for office bound staff and for WFH employees. Both of these groups of employees must have the same contracts of employment, but with the WFH employees, for instance, there may be customised WFH addendums to the contract that make provision for the special circumstances of those employees. In most respects the same terms and conditions will apply to all employees, with the exception of some, where separate terms are enclosed.

6.4.3 Contracts of employment must be monitored, revisited and as necessary updated. In particular, the following aspects could be relevant:

- **Variation clauses**

  Variation clauses (i.e. changes to a contract) may need to be relaxed in order to be more flexible and in order for new conditions and terms to be implemented rapidly in the interests of the employer and employees.

- **Working arrangements**

  Working arrangements, reporting schedules, absenteeism management and hours of work are just some of the issues that need to be revised and incorporated. A new Employee Handbook can be introduced in this regard.

- **Medical testing**

  Medical testing (with reference to sections 6, 7 and 8 of the EEA) is prohibited unless legislation requires the same, or if it is "justifiable" in light of the circumstances. The consent of the employee is immaterial, in other words employee consent is not possible. The provisions of the National Health Act, especially with reference to "medical treatment", also comes into play and permits the administration of vaccines. With regard to the general prohibition (against testing) contained in section 7 of the EAA, employers can legally justify medical testing in light of *"employment conditions, social policy, the fair distribution of employee benefits or the inherent requirements of the specific job"*, i.e. with or without the consent of the employee, medical testing is still possible, depending on how this is crafted.

Medical testing refers to both a test or an inquiry to confirm whether an employee has a medical condition. Section 7 of the EEA therefore does not prohibit a mandatory workplace vaccination policy.

The law in respect of compulsory vaccinations still needs to be developed in South Africa, beyond the EEA's provision related to "where legislation permits or recognises the testing", and the public interest concept will provide for a catapult in this regard, inclusive of the possible revision of individual rights in order to protect society at large.

In the USA, for instance, mandatory vaccination is permissible for adults to preserve public health and safety (*Jacobsen v. Massachusetts 197 U.S. 11* (1905) - United States Supreme Court).

The following factors in South Africa can mitigate against compulsory vaccination legislation and/or policies:

1. Medical reasons.
2. Safety concerns.
3. Religious, cultural or philosophical objections.

The following 'vaccination clause' is suggested for Contract of Employment purposes:

VACCINATIONS

The employee agrees that it may become necessary, dependent on prevailing safety and health, socio-economic and legal (inclusive of statutory) requirements, for the employee to be vaccinated in response to a health threat that could compromise the business of the employer;

The employee also agrees that the employer can validly require the employee to be vaccinated dependent on circumstances and/or the needs of the employer;

A process of mandatory vaccination shall be in compliance with constitutional and statutory prescriptions;

Provided that the employee is at liberty, at any time, to be vaccinated on a voluntary basis and to provide the employer with proof of such vaccination administered.

- **Medical examination**

  The employer may require the employee to undergo a medical examination that is related to the employee's job and based on a business necessity, where the employer deems the examination necessary to confirm an employee's fitness for duty or eligibility for sick, medical or disability leave. The employer may also require such an examination to determine the employee's eligibility to return from any sick leave, especially where the employee is returning having exhausted available sick leave, or to determine an employee's ability to return to full service from a recuperative status. The examination is normally held at the employer's expense.

  The employer cannot force the employee to be examined by a doctor, whether it is the employee's own doctor or an employer appointed one. However, in the event of a contractual clause authorising the employer to require the employee to attend a medical examination, a refusal to comply without good reason can amount to breach of contract. As a result, the employee could be disciplined and/or dealt with in terms of an applicable incapacity and ill-health procedure, in order to possibly terminate services.

  Any medical reports are confidential, and will have to be considered and processed in terms of the provisions of the Protection of Personal Information Act.

  The responsible employer will not in isolation of circumstances and without valid reason demand that the employee submits to a medical examination, and is entitled to come to an adverse inference should an employee, without valid reason, refuse to cooperate.

  The following contractual clause for inclusion in contracts of employment is proposed:

  - ***"Medical examination.*** *The employee will, whenever the company deems it to be necessary for employment contract compliance purposes, and in order to establish the employee's capacity to comply with duties, undergo a medical examination at the expense of the company. The examination shall normally be conducted by a medical practitioner nominated and appointed by the company in order to assist in establishing the employee's general health and well-being for the purposes of employment. The unreasonable refusal of the employee to comply with such an instruction may constitute breach of contract."*

- **Physical searching and alcohol/drug and/or polygraph testing**

  These are contractual obligations that are synonymous with the workplace and are also in accordance with the OHSA provisions, with the exception of polygraph testing. The rights to privacy and self-incrimination is at play here, thus care needs to be taken in respect of implementation techniques, based on a valid reason for taking action and due process.

- **POPI Act**

  The provisions of the Protection of Personal Information Act (POPI), which was set out to regulate personal employee information, requires business owners to process such personal information according to stated processing conditions. The provisions of POPI (in a health context) apply when requesting an employee or potential employees to make disclosures regarding their medical or vaccination history, as such information constitutes "special personal information".

- **RICA***

  The RICA Act (Regulation of Interception of Communications and Provisions of Communication Related Information Act, 2002) read with the POPI Act (referred to hereinabove) is applicable to the electronic monitoring of employee communications and also provides for the legalities of monitoring employees' physical movements and activities.

  With available surveillance technology software, employers are in a position to track live locations; monitor and track internet, cell phone, email and video activities; and take screenshots of employees' desktops remotely. (Also see the Sample Electronic Communications Policy and Procedure contained in the Toolkit section of this book.)

  *RICA has been repealed by the Constitutional Court except for some interim relief, with the result that effectively Parliament has until 2023 to revise the Act and to establish sufficient safeguards to protect the public. The invalidity of RICA has in other words been suspended until 2023.

  In addition, RICA allows for employee monitoring if:

  - the employee consents to such monitoring;
  - the monitoring or interception occurs in the normal course of business; and
  - interception is carried out by a person who is party to the same communication.

Employers should ensure that they obtain prior written consent (for monitoring and interception) in contracts of employment, and to include reference to the processing of personal information (POPI) and interception of communication (RICA) in the contract or addendum thereto.

6.5 **Societal Inputs into Contracts**

The following diagram is provided to highlight societal inputs into contracts of employment, which also makes such contracts the subject of change:

THE CONTRACT OF EMPLOYMENT - POST 2020 SOCIO-ECONOMIC POLITICAL INPUTS, CHANGES AND ADAPTATIONS

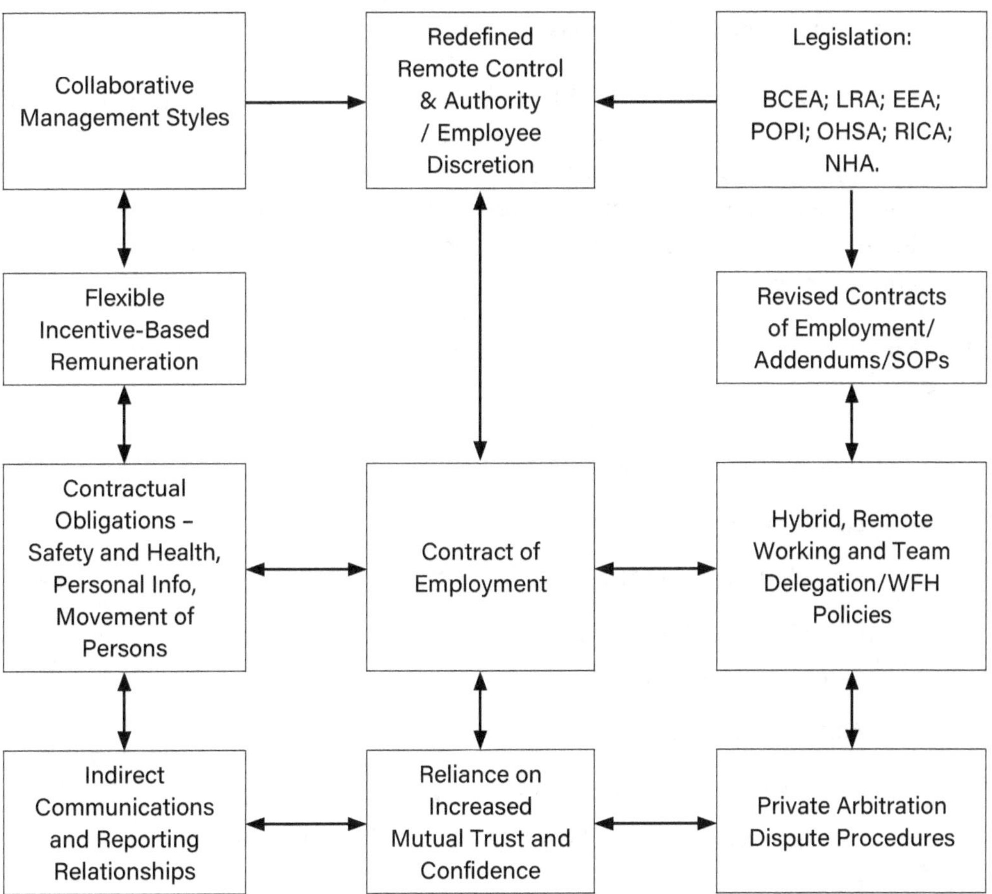

NOTES:

The diagram illustrates some of the compelling changes that contracts of employment need to accommodate. The success and competitiveness of a company's "culture", i.e. the values, beliefs, human 'capital', business methods and profitability recipe of the employer, is of significant importance, as increasingly a collaborative management style will be required.

6.6 Managing the Home Office

6.6.1 Some employees are better suited than others to work from home and employers need to take cognisance of this.

6.6.2 WFH employees have constitutional and other rights to privacy, inclusive of access rights to their homes, that need to be considered and respected. The employer has a corresponding right to ensure and be informed that the home office is appropriately managed in order to be optimally productive. As always, the employer's employment policies and procedures are applicable remotely and to the home office.

6.6.3 Some employer problem areas in respect of WFH are cited as follows:

- Poor work performance.
- Breaches of Restraint of Trade.
- Desertion or abscondment.
- Unauthorised absence.
- Defiance of instructions.
- Plotting with competitors.
- Alcohol and/or drug abuse.
- Depression or mental conditions.
- Safety and health, and the health status of the employee.
- Salary disputes.
- Disputes in respect of WFH costs.
- Dishonesty and deviousness.

- Lack of transparency.
- Pandemic compliance monitoring.
- Falsification of records.
- Domestic issues and/or poor work conditions.

6.6.4 In addition to employment contract obligations and duties, and as a normal daily activity, an employer must attend to:

- the creation and establishment of a logical and practical WFH model, using the contract of employment, SOEs, policy guidelines and applicable legislation as the framework;
- a collaborative and consensus seeking process to get "buy-in" from all parties, i.e. employees, supervisors and management;
- making the trust component a central feature of the company culture by stressing reciprocity and the maintenance of confidence in the abilities of employees; and
- allowing WFH employees to work independently subject to daily monitoring and checks and balances, through the process of decentralised, indirect management, and control and authority.

To place this chapter in context, the following important documentation contained in the Toolkit must be considered:

- WFH Policy and Procedure
- KPAs and Performance Agreement
- Poor Work Performance Policy and Procedure
- Remuneration and Incentive Scheme Guidelines
- Electronic Communications Policy and Procedure
- Alcohol and Drug Usage; Remedial Policy and Procedures
- Health and Safety, and Medical Treatment Policy Guidelines

CHAPTER 7

REPUDIATION, BREACHES OF CONTRACT AND REMEDIAL RIGHTS

"Be sure to understand the terms of any contract, before you sign." (Lailah Gifty Akita)

'Breach of contract' is a legal term that describes the violation of an agreement when one party fails to fulfil its promises made in the contract. In this chapter such breaches of contract are dealt with, including some of the forms of breach akin to employment relations, inclusive of remedial rights and responses.

7.1 Introduction

The most fundamental element of the employment contract is that the relationship between employer and employee is in essence one of trust and confidence, and any conduct clearly inconsistent therewith entitles the innocent party to cancel the agreement.

The obligation and contractual duty not to destroy the employment relationship cuts both ways, and it is implied that either party shall not conduct itself in a manner likely to damage or destroy the relationship of trust and confidence. Loss of confidence in the ability of the employee to comply with his/her duties and contractual obligations equates to a loss of trust, entitling the employer to withdraw from the contract of employment on the basis of repudiation.

An assessment of whether an employee, or employer for that matter, has breached the trust relationship should normally consist of a structured, well thought out investigation, in order to establish if, in fact, the employment relationship has broken down irretrievably. Such assessment is not necessary in the event of patently obvious gross and material breaches of contract, for instance in the event of admitted embezzlement, dishonesty or theft.

A "material" (that is a gross or serious act or omission) breach of contract by either party occurs when one of them fails to abide by the terms of the agreement. Examples of such repudiatory conduct would be an employer failing to pay wages as agreed, denying an employee benefits that the employee is entitled to, and the premature cancellation of the contract. An employee, on the other hand, will be liable for breach of contract where the employee is dishonest, deserts and seeks employment elsewhere, where confidential information is disclosed, or where the employer suffers damages as a result of the irresponsible actions of the employee, and so forth.

As each employment contract is unique and different, a breach of contract may be found for several different reasons. One of the benefits of reducing the agreement to a written contract is that there may be written evidence of exactly what each party had agreed to in respect of their respective rights and duties. So, in the event of a real or perceived problem, and/or suspected and/or alleged breach and/or infringement of rights, the first step inevitably will be to check on the contents of the contract in order to ascertain the respective duties and obligations of the parties.

7.2 Material Breach of Contract and Repudiation

Repudiation is the technical term for a serious or "material" breach of contract. As explained hereinabove, this occurs when the conduct of one party - either the employer or employee - demonstrates an intention to no longer be bound by the terms of the contract, or to fulfil it in a manner materially inconsistent with their obligations.

Such breach or repudiation gives the innocent party the right to either cancel the contract by accepting the repudiation, or, if the innocent party decides not to accept the repudiation, the contract will continue to apply. In each case alternative remedies apply, that is a claim for damages or the insistence on specific performance.

Repudiation by a party does not in itself terminate the contract, so whilst the contract is intact, it gives the innocent party the choice of either accepting that the breach has brought the contract between them to an end, or rejecting the breach and seeking an order for specific performance, demanding that the other party complies with its obligations.

7.3 Examples of Repudiatory Conduct

Examples of employer conduct that may constitute repudiation include:

- failing to pay the employee the agreed remuneration;

- making unilateral changes to employment contract terms;
- reducing an employee's remuneration or withdrawing a contractual benefit (e.g. a motor vehicle) without consent;
- making changes to an employee's role resulting in a significant reduction in status and/or responsibilities;
- making unilateral changes to the employee's core duties and KPAs; and
- a failure to provide a safe and healthy workplace.

Examples of what may constitute repudiatory conduct by an employee include:

- absenteeism and not turning up for work;
- failure to comply with reporting instructions;
- poor work performance and failure to achieve targets;
- desertion;
- resigning part way through a project or fixed-term contract;
- refusing to comply adequately with KPAs;
- engaging in unacceptable social media communications;
- bringing the name of the employer into disrepute;
- incompetence;
- resigning for ulterior motives;
- breach of restraint of trade or confidentiality agreement; and
- bad faith conduct.

The following example, citing desertion, will assist practically to illustrate the above: the employee is repudiating the contract as he/she deserts from employment with the intention never to return, having taken up employment elsewhere. The employer decides to accept the repudiation and is entitled to step out of the contract as a result, and to claim damages from the employee. The employer under such circumstances had decided to accept the repudiation of the contract, instead of holding the employee to remedy the breach through specific performance. The remedy of specific performance would have been inappropriate as a result of the personal services rendered, as well as the irretrievable breakdown in the employment and trust relationship.

Conversely, in circumstances where the employee has repeatedly been warned to improve their performance in order to achieve agreed targets, the employer can demand specific performance in order to achieve those targets, although the employee is in breach of the employment contract.

To sum up:

7.3.1 The employer's remedies in response to repudiation are as follows:

- **Summary dismissal**

  Termination of the contract and dismissal provides for the most common employer response to an employee's breach of contract, for instance in the case of misconduct. Summary dismissal means dismissal without the giving of notice. The LRA overrides the common law and prescribes that the employer must comply with fair dismissal procedures, inclusive of substantive and procedural fairness.

- **Specific performance**

  As a result of practicalities and the personal nature of the services rendered by the employee, inclusive of the possible loss of trust and confidence normally associated with a dismissal for misconduct, it is unlikely that specific performance will be ordered against the employee, except for special circumstances.

- **Damages**

  An employer is entitled to claim damages, inclusive of contractual and incidental damages, from an employee for conduct that may have caused them damage, which will be discussed below.

- **Cancellation of contract**

  Under certain circumstances, the employer can also cancel the contract by tendering the requisite notice period.

7.3.2 Remedies available to the employee also include the acceptance of repudiation and a claim for damages, or alternatively, the insistence on specific performance by the employer.

- **Specific performance**

  Due to the personal nature of a contract of employment and the possibility that the employment relationship has been compromised, common law orders for specific performance will only be granted in exceptional circumstances.

7.3.3 Damages

An employee may claim actual damages and financial compensation suffered as a result of the breach of contract by the employer, irrespective of whether such employee elects to terminate the contract or to continue with it. Importantly, employees have a duty to mitigate their loss, which means, in effect, that they are obliged to look for another job.

The amount for contractual damages that an employee can claim for unlawful breach of contract depends on the nature of the contract, i.e. whether it is an indefinite or a fixed-term contract.

If the contract is for a fixed period, it may be terminated by the employer only if the employee is in material breach. If the contract is unlawfully terminated by the employer before the expiry date, the employee may claim the equivalent of the amount that would have been earned between the date of contract and the date of termination, less any earnings received.

The employee must still prove the damages so claimed, however, and they are not automatically entitled to the salary that would have been earned, had it not been for the unlawful termination of contract. The latter is in accordance with the principle of the mitigation of losses.

In the event of an indefinite contract with no termination date, the employee will only be able to claim for salary in respect of the notice period that would have been applicable.

The Labour Court has the discretion to award damages under the LRA and the EEA, as this function is circumscribed by the phrase "in any circumstances contemplated by the Act". The LRA does not expressly provide for awards of damages, but the mention of "damages" in s158(1)(a)(vi) of the LRA and s50(2)(b) of the EEA means that employees may claim damages as opposed to, or in addition to, compensation (as provide for in section 193 of the LRA). The CCMA has no jurisdiction to arbitrate in respect of claims for damages, and is limited to considering and making awards in response to claims for compensation.

A claim for damages in the Labour Court will only succeed on the basis of actual, proven damages claimed through a rigorous "nuts and bolts" exercise, where the loss of hard cash or anticipated, guaranteed income can be proven.

Claims for non-financial items such as mental stress, frustration, annoyance, reputational harm, hurt feelings and general prejudice will not be readily considered.

Such sentimental damages normally infringe on the absolute and primordial rights of dignity, liberty or reputation, inclusive of defamation.

The term "damages" is normally used to describe an amount of money awarded to a claimant to make good the losses occasioned by an unlawful action by another, for example a former employee who poached a key member of staff; a trade union that burnt down the company offices; an employee who was unlawfully downgraded to a lesser salary scale; or an employee who was dismissed without reason on the basis of false information.

As stated above, the employee must prove the losses claimed, that this could have been avoided, and that the same was the direct result of repudiation. Further, they must prove that there was a mitigation of such losses, or at least an attempt to mitigate those losses.

In addition, in *Aaron's Whale Rock Trust v Murray and Roberts Ltd and Another* [1992] 3 All SA 390 (C), it was held that:

> *"Where damages can be assessed with exact mathematical precision, a plaintiff is expected to adduce sufficient evidence to meet this requirement. Where, as is the case here, this cannot be done, the plaintiff must lead such evidence as is available to it (but of adequate sufficiency) so as to enable the Court to quantify his damages and to make an appropriate award in his favour. The Court must not be faced with an exercise in guesswork; what is required of a plaintiff is that he should put before the Court enough evidence from which it can, albeit with difficulty, compensate him by an award of money as a fair approximation of his mathematically unquantifiable loss."*

In *Esso Standard SA (Pty) Ltd v Katz* 1981 (1) SA 964 (A), the following was held regarding the necessity of producing proof of damages suffered:

> *"In the present case it might be said with some justification that the plaintiff should have sought the assistance of an accountant. He failed to do so, but it does not follow that he should be non-suited. Whether or not a plaintiff should be non-suited depends on whether he has adduced all the evidence reasonably available to him... and is a problem which has engaged the attention of the Courts from time to time."*

The court went on to quote with approval the following passage in *Hersman v Shapiro and Co* 1926 TPD 367:

"Monetary damage having been suffered, it is necessary for the Court to assess the amount and make the best use it can of the evidence before it. There are cases where the assessment by the Court is very little more than an estimate; but even so, if it is certain that pecuniary damage has been suffered, the Court is bound to award damages. It is not so bound in the case where evidence is available to the plaintiff which he has not produced; in those circumstances the Court is justified in giving, and does give, absolution from the instance. But where the best evidence available has been produced, though it is not entirely of a conclusive character and does not permit of a mathematical calculation of the damages suffered, still, if it is the best evidence available, the Court must use it and arrive at a conclusion based upon it."

CHAPTER 8

DISPUTES AND DISPUTE PROCEDURES

This chapter examines applicable common law as well as statutory dispute procedures, in particular disputes about contracts of employment, remedies available in the event of repudiation, claims for damages, and the structure of a statement of claim for the purposes of section 77(3) of the BCEA.

8.1 Introduction

Common law actions in response to repudiation (material breaches of contract), as discussed in Chapter 7, are to be distinguished from actions instituted by means of the provisions of the LRA, BCEA or EAA for various employment breaches, whether it is for unfair dismissal, unfair labour practices, or breaches of contract, to name but a few of the possibilities.

In the event that employees institute action under the LRA, they are seeking, albeit statutory specific performance or compensation for infringements of their constitutional rights, by means of reinstatement or compensation orders as provided for. The Labour Court arbitrators are empowered to grant either forms of relief but different considerations will apply. Section 194 of the LRA provides for the latter and is not to be confused with a damage claim.

The LRA, in the event of unfair dismissal, provides for the primary remedy of reinstatement or compensation. "Reinstatement" and "compensation" are mutually exclusive remedies and both cannot be awarded. However, the reinstated employee is in principle entitled to retrospective back pay and the latter must not be confused with compensation. The compensation that an employee may be entitled to is over and above any other claims that such employee may have, for instance claims in respect of severance pay or damages for breach of contract.

In addition to actions that the employer and employee could have against each other, the employer is vicariously liable for a wrong committed by his employee during the course or scope of his or her employment; this means acts committed by the employee in the exercise of the functions for which s/he was appointed, including such acts as were reasonably necessary to carry out instructions.

The employer is not, however, liable where the employee committed an intentional wrong entirely for his or her own purpose, unrelated to the contract of employment.

Those who seek damages under common law have two specific remedies for breach of contract: an order for specific performance and/or an award of damages. The latter was dealt with in Chapter 7 of this book.

The statutory compensation remedy provided for in the LRA, as stated hereinabove, must not be confused with a claim for common law damages, and the aggrieved employee is entitled to launch separate proceedings to be heard at different forums for both compensation as well as damages. In respect of compensation, the LRA provides as follows:

"194 Limits on compensation

(1) The compensation awarded to an employee whose dismissal is found to be unfair either because the employer did not prove that the reason for dismissal was a fair reason relating to the employee's conduct or capacity or the employer's operational requirements or the employer did not follow a fair procedure, or both, must be just and equitable in all the circumstances, but may not be more that the equivalent of 12 months' remuneration on the date of dismissal.

(2) The compensation awarded to an employee whose dismissal is automatically unfair must be just and equitable in all the circumstances, but may not be more than the equivalent of 24 months' remuneration calculated at the employee's rate of remuneration at the time of dismissal."

8.2 Disputes Concerning Contracts of Employment

Section 77A(e) of the BCEA is effectively an extension of section 77(3) and states that when a court considers a matter regarding a contract of employment, that court has the power to make an order for specific performance, damages and/or compensation. This provision gives the Labour Court equal powers and rights to those of civil courts, where terms or conditions in contracts of employment are in dispute or in the event of a breach of the terms of a contract.

Section 77(3) of the BCEA accordingly gives the Labour Court concurrent jurisdiction with the civil courts to hear and determine any matter concerning a contract of employment, irrespective of whether any basic condition of employment constitutes a term of that contract. The intention is to give the Labour Court jurisdiction to entertain purely contractual claims, as opposed to those arising from statutory rights, i.e. the right to not be unfairly dismissed.

Section 77A(e)of the BCEA also means that the Labour Court is clothed with jurisdiction to hear contractual matters, and reads as follows: *"...including an order... making a determination that it considers reasonable on any matter concerning a contract of employment in terms of section 77(3), which determination may include an order for specific performance, an award of damages or an award of compensation."*

A claim under this provision must therefore allege a breach of contract, as opposed to an allegation of unfairness. Sometimes there will be little to distinguish these claims, especially where the contract incorporates the provisions of labour legislation. A restraint of trade agreement is a matter concerning a contract of employment, as envisaged by section 77 of the BCEA, and accordingly falls within the jurisdiction of the Labour Court.

Claims of breach of contract need to focus on contractual breaches *per se* and must avoid resorting to allegations of unfairness and unfair labour practice, which could possibly compromise the claim in respect of CCMA jurisdiction, as well as an inappropriate course of action, that is that the matter should have been referred as an unfair labour practice dispute.

The BCEA is devoid of specific provisions for the prosecution of contractual claims in the Labour Court. Such matters may be brought in terms of the Rules of the Labour Court, by way of Application (Rule 7), if the applicant does not foresee significant disputes of fact, or by way of Referral (Rule 6) if material factual disputes are possible and foreseeable.

A STATEMENT OF CLAIM IN TERMS OF RULE 6 OF THE RULES OF THE LABOUR COURT WILL CONSIST OF THE FOLLOWING:

1. THE TITLE OF THE MATTER INCLUSIVE OF THE PARTIES IN DISPUTE AND THE CASE NUMBER.
2. A CLEAR AND CONCISE STATEMENT RELATED TO THE MATERIAL FACTS IN CHRONOLOGICAL ORDER, THE CONDUCT COMPLAINED OF AS WELL AS PARTICULARS OF BREACH OF CONTRACT.
3. A CLEAR AND CONCISE STATEMENT OF THE LEGAL ISSUES THAT ARISE FROM THE MATERIAL FACTS INCLUSIVE OF APPLICABLE LAW, IN ORDER TO ENABLE ANY OPPOSING PARTY TO REPLY IN AN INFORMED MANNER.
4. THE RELIEF CLAIMED.
5. A SCHEDULE OF DOCUMENTS TO BE RELIED UPON.
6. PROOF OF SERVICE ON THE OTHER SIDE.

The following diagram provides for a flowchart in respect of the section 77(3) dispute process:

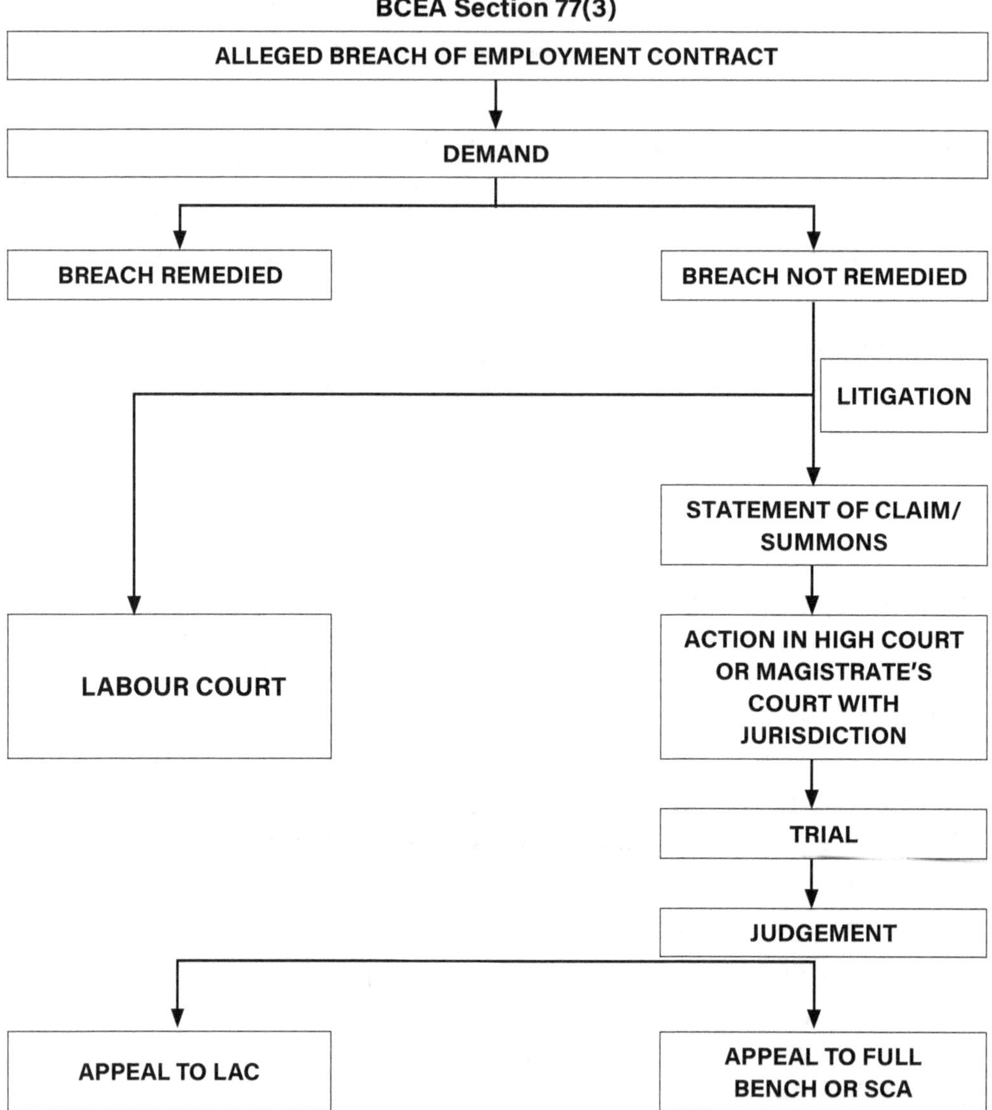

8.3 Unilateral Changes to Contract Terms and Conditions

Contract law determines that terms and conditions of employment must be agreed to, and that the same can only be changed with the consent of the parties. In some sophisticated contracts a 'unilateral changes clause' can feature which means that the employer can vary the terms of the contract unilaterally, especially if such change is in the 'substantial interest' of the employer.

By enforcing unilateral changes without adequate preventative measures in place, the existing contract of employment is effectively terminated, and substituted by a new contract.

In addition to the available common law remedies for repudiation and breaches of contract related to unilateral changes to contract terms and conditions, the following statutory mechanisms are applicable, over and above common law provisions, as follows:

- Section 64(4) of the LRA provides that the employee can refer the dispute to the CCMA and require the employer not to unilaterally implement the change, or to restore the status quo ante;
- Section 186(e) of the LRA, constructive dismissal, can also be alleged by the employee;
- Section 186(2) of the LRA, unfair labour practice, can also be utilized where employment benefits are reduced;
- Sections 189 and 189A of the LRA give the employer the right to resort to organisational restructuring and retrenchment proceedings in response to justified, necessary changes to contracts of employment that are rejected by employees.
- Section 186(1)(e) of the LRA provides for constructive dismissal claims, for instance, if the employee resigns because of the unilateral reduction of an agreed salary or any other change introduced by the employer, possibly intended to create intolerable working conditions.

The South African courts correctly emphasise the individual terms of each contract (inclusive of variation clauses) when assessing legal ramifications and enforceability issues. Unfortunately, the resultant judgments over a period of many years have lacked consistency, with the result that a relatively sparse body of case law has developed, with little attention paid to the balance between employee rights and commercial rationale.

8.4 Statutory Remedies for Unfair Dismissals

This book is concerned with employment contractual rights and obligations, and not with the consequences of unfair dismissal. However, the relevant sections in respect of remedies and compensation in response to findings of statutory unfair dismissal are quoted as follows, keeping in mind that "damages" and "compensation" are two different things and not mutually exclusive. This means that an employee can claim for both damages as well as for compensation, albeit at different forums.

*"**193 Remedies for unfair dismissal and unfair labour practice***

(1) If the Labour Court or an arbitrator appointed in terms of this Act finds that a dismissal is unfair, the Court or the arbitrator may-

(a) order the employer to reinstate the employee from any date not earlier than the date of dismissal;

(b) order the employer to re-employ the employee, either in the work in which the employee was employed before the dismissal or in other reasonably suitable work on any terms and from any date not earlier than the date of dismissal; or

(c) order the employer to pay compensation to the employee.

(2) The Labour Court or the arbitrator must require the employer to reinstate or re-employ the employee unless-

(a) the employee does not wish to be reinstated or re-employed;

(b) the circumstances surrounding the dismissal are such that a continued employment relationship would be intolerable;

(c) it is not reasonably practicable for the employer to reinstate or re-employ the employee; or

(d) the dismissal is unfair only because the employer did not follow a fair procedure.

(3) If a dismissal is automatically unfair or, if a dismissal based on the employer's operational requirements is found to be unfair, the Labour Court in addition may make any other order that it considers appropriate in the circumstances.

(4) An arbitrator appointed in terms of this Act may determine any unfair labour practice dispute referred to the arbitrator, on terms that the arbitrator deems reasonable, which may include ordering reinstatement, re-employment or compensation."

8.5 The Courts and Statutory Mechanisms

An alleged breach of the terms of a contract of employment, unfair dismissal claims and others are dealt with through creations of statutes and primarily through the mechanisms of the CCMA, the Labour Court, the Labour Appeal Court and the Constitutional Court. Private arbitration is a much neglected and under-utilised form of dispute resolution, which could be highly effective in respect of both the often very lengthy durations of litigation and associated legal costs.

In some cases, the High Courts and Labour Courts could have concurrent jurisdiction, for instance in claims related to contracts of employment and damages.

Again, it ought to be borne in mind that claims for damages must not be conflated with rules for compensation that the Labour Court or CCMA can order.

Compensation, as provided for in section 194 (see above) of the LRA, means a statutorily prescribed sum of money to compensate for the unfairness of the dismissal so perpetrated in certain instances. This is something entirely different to a claim for damages, which a claimant is required to prove.

8.6 **Private Arbitration**

'Private arbitration' is a term often used in commercial, construction and labour circles for arbitrations conducted under the Arbitration Act 42 of 1965, as opposed to those conducted under the LRA or related statutes. Nothing prevents parties from deciding on alternatives to statutory dispute resolution procedures by agreeing to resort to private arbitration, and that an arbitrator will resolve a dispute between them.

This applies in respect of particular disputes, or disputes in general, and whether the disputes would otherwise have to be referred to the Labour Court or to the CCMA for statutory arbitration. Private arbitration may take place only with the agreement of all parties involved, and are normally conducted for deserving cases dependent on circumstances.

The process of private arbitration provides for a more expeditious resolution of disputes, and will undoubtedly become increasingly popular in view of court cases loads, severe administrative problems, and a shortage of funds, which all means that it could take a considerable period of time for matters to be brought to conclusion by means of statutory forums. In addition, safety and health considerations could play a major role in moving away from statutory dispute resolution mechanisms.

The option of private arbitration may become increasingly attractive in view of the relatively speedy resolution of disputes and the finalisation of matters that otherwise could be dragged out for years in courts of law. The latter, inclusive of the entire judicial system, are increasingly coming under pressure as a result of socio-economic and political circumstances, inclusive of the relative scarcity of resources and of professional office bearers.

CONCLUSION

The contract of employment is central to the employment relationship, and in fact forms the very basis of economic activity in South Africa.

Without carefully thought-out and documented contracts, employment policies and procedures, an organisation could lose everything it stands for - profitability and a competitive edge in growing, sustaining its operations, fairness in employment practices, and fundamental principles which employers and employees should be committed to.

A contract of employment is a contract of trust which bonds and cements the parties to their intentions, contractual duties and responsibilities. To avoid stagnation, the contract should be regularly updated and reviewed to ensure that it remains relevant and that the terms continue to be current and applicable.

Above all, the terms of a contract of employment must be clear, concise and unambiguous, understandable and in plain language for it to be accessible and meaningful to both parties. If not, the relationship will be compromised.

The increased demands of changed socio-economic and political circumstances, technology and the fourth industrial revolution, inclusive of universal drastic changes in work, communication and employment practices, obliges employers to adopt a fresh if not alert stance in respect of the importance of the contract of employment, as the origin and source of its economic activities.

TOOLKIT

SAMPLE CONTRACTS, GUIDELINES, POLICIES, PROCEDURES AND STATUTORY REGULATIONS

SAMPLE
BASIC CONTRACT OF EMPLOYMENT

MADE AND ENTERED INTO BY AND BETWEEN

______________________	______________________
(name of Employer)	(with address at)

Herein represented by ______________________ duly authorized hereto (hereinafter referred to as the *"Employer")*

AND

______________________	______________________
(name of Employee)	(with address at)
______________________	______________________
(identity number)	(mobile number)

(hereinafter referred to as the *"Employee")*

For further purposes of this agreement, the male shall import the female and vice versa, and reference to "company" shall include reference to "employer".

WHEREAS

1.1 The Company appoints the employee to provide services and the employee accepts such appointment by the Company.

1.2 The employee is able to provide the services required by the Company and warrants that he is suitably organized, qualified and experienced in the provision of the services referred to and required in terms of this contract.

1.3 The parties hereto wish to record and reduce this agreement into writing, in order to constitute a written contract of employment.

WHEREBY THE PARTIES AGREE AS FOLLOWS:

1. **APPOINTMENT, DUTIES AND GUARANTEES**

   1.1 It is hereby confirmed that the employee has been offered and has accepted employment with the Company as a ______________________ (job title) at ______________________ (premises/site)

1.2 The Company hereby appoints the employee to provide services within the scope and duties of the appointment, as set out in **Annexure A** - agreed Key Performance Areas ("KPA's") and achievement of targets (**Optional Clause**). See item 9 of the Toolkit.

1.3 The employee implicitly agrees ad promises that:

1.3.1 He is competent to perform contractual obligations and the work employed for;

1.3.2 He must perform all functions and activities assigned to the best of his ability and in an efficient manner;

1.3.3 He must perform duties in accordance with Company policy, guidelines and instructions, custom and practice, as well as implied understandings;

1.3.4 He guarantees that agreed performance and output targets required by the Company will be met and achieved, and further agrees that underperformance, inclusive of inefficiency and incompetence, or the inability to achieve set standards, could lead to the termination of this contract.

1.3.5 The employee unconditionally confirms, recognizes and supports the complete flexibility of jobs and duties and will comply with all reasonable instructions, inclusive of the performance of additional duties and tasks, as and when required by the Company.

1.4 The core of the employee's obligations is the duty to respect the employer and to obey and to comply with all reasonable instructions, to act in the interests of the employer and not to be guilty of conduct that could destroy the trust relationship, or which in any way could compromise the same.

1.5 This is a full time appointment, and the employee shall devote his full commitment, energy and attention to the Company's business.

The employee shall not at any time during the continuance of this contract be directly or indirectly engaged, concerned or interested whether for reward or otherwise, in any other trade, business or profession without the explicit written consent of the employer.

1.6 The Company's employment policies, rules and regulations are provided for under separate cover.

2. DURATION

2.1 This agreement will continue for an indefinite period until it has been cancelled in terms hereof, or in accordance with the provisions of law.

3. REMUNERATION AND CONDITIONS OF EMPLOYMENT

3.1 The employee will receive a basic monthly salary of ____________ (cost-to-company), which monthly salary shall be paid on the ____ day of each month into a bank account so nominated by the employee, payable by electronic fund transfer *("EFT")*.

3.2 The employee's statutory conditions of employment, inclusive of leave regulations, are primarily regulated by the provisions of Basic Conditions of Employment Act ("BCEA"), which will be provided under separate cover.

3.3 Normal hours of work on, or off Company premises, are as follows:

3.3.1 Monday to Friday - 08h00 - 16h30

3.3.2 Dependent on agreed hybrid or flexi-time arrangements, hours of work are subject to change and could include Saturday and/or Sunday work, as well as overtime work sometimes at short notice.

3.4 The employee unconditionally agrees to deductions from remuneration as follows:

▪ Reimbursement of personal, study, medical or other loans; ▪ Salary in lieu of time not worked and/or services not provided; ▪ Failure to provide statutory or contractual notice period; ▪ Overpayments; ▪ Statutory deductions, UIF, PAYE and Workman's Compensation deductions;	▪ Court/Garnishee orders; ▪ Loss or damage to property, or suffered as a result of theft or fraudulent conduct; ▪ Housing costs; ▪ Training costs; ▪ Meals/canteen facilities. ▪ Any other amount agreed to, subject to section 34 of the BCEA

4. SHORT TIME

4.1. Should the employer be unable to productively employ the employee for the ordinary hours of work per week due to slackness of trade, shortage of raw materials, a general breakdown of plant or machinery caused by an accident or any other unforeseen emergency, the employer may implement short time during, but not exceeding the period of unforeseen circumstances. For a period of short time the employee will be remunerated for the hours worked. Where practically possible, written notice regarding the implementation of short time must be given to the employee in writing at least 24 hours prior to, or less if the circumstances are more urgent of the date of which short time will be implemented.

5. GENERAL

5.1 Health and Safety

5.1.1 The statutory as well as contractual obligations to provide for a safe and healthy workplace rest primarily on the employer, with the active assistance and cooperation of the employee.

5.1.2 The statutory duties and general duty of care referred to hereinabove are applicable to, on as well as off Company premises, and are equally applicable to hybrid, remote and work-from-home practices.

5.1.3 The Company agrees that the employee has constitutionally protected rights, such as freedom and security of person, and privacy as well as the right to religious and cultural freedom. It is agreed that none of the rights referred to hereinabove are absolute.

5.1.4 It is agreed that Statutory Regulations as well as Company policies, rules and guidelines in respect of the safety and health of employees, inclusive of the population at large, must be taken into consideration in order to achieve, and to further enhance a safe and healthy work environment.

5.1.5 It is further agreed that disregard of safety and health rules and protocols, and deliberate and/or negligent breach of, inclusive of obstructive conduct of same, and the refusal to comply with reasonable instructions, will constitute material breach of contract and could result in the dismissal of the employee.

5.1 Force Majeure

Neither party will be liable for the delay or failure to perform any obligation and or undertaking in terms of this contract in the event and to the extent that such delay or failure is caused by force majeure including but not limited to an act of God, fire, lightening, earthquake, explosion, flood, emergency, insurrection, civil disorder, war, military operations, pandemic, act of terrorism or the declaration of a national disaster or state of emergency.

5.2 Company Rules and Regulations

5.2.1 Schedule 8 to the Labour Relationship Act: "A Code of Good Conduct – Dismissal" is applicable as a Guideline Code to this agreement in respect of –

5.2.1.1 Disciplinary measures;
5.2.1.2 Dismissal;
5.2.1.1 Probation (if applicable);
5.2.1.2 Poor Work Performance;
5.2.1.3 Incapacity and ill-health;
5.2.1.4 Medical incapacity.

5.2.2 Company specific rules, policies and procedures inclusive of rules of conduct, are available under separate cover.

5.2.3 The employee agrees that it is necessary for the employer to implement measures and procedures on an on-going basis, in order to protect and to further the employer's business, as well as the safety, health and wellbeing of fellow employees and customers. The employee further agrees to and gives his irrevocable consent to any examination and/or testing for such purpose, including, but not limited to:

5.2.3.1 Medical examinations and/or testing, excluding testing prohibited by law;

5.2.3.2 Blood, urine or breathalyser/alcohol tests;

5.2.3.3 Drug and or any illegal substance testing;

5.2.3.4 Polygraph testing;

5.2.3.5 Fingerprint examination and/or security clearances.

5.2.4 The employee agrees to searching of his person or property in the event of a reasonable suspicion of misconduct and/or as part of access control measures to the premises of the employer.

5.2.5 The employee is aware of, agrees and consents to the monitoring of any premises and/or vehicles from where the employee may be conducting work and duties, by means of electronic surveillance and/or surveillance equipment and/or similar equipment, provided that such surveillance complies with statutory requirements.

5.3 **Variations and Changes to Contract**

5.3.1 With the exception of clauses 6.3.2 and 6.3.3 hereof, no provision of this contract may be amended, substituted or varied, and no provision may be added to or incorporated in this contract, except by an agreement in writing between the parties.

5.3.2 The employee agrees and consents to the following variations and changes to this contract, to be effected by the Company, from time to time:

5.3.2.1 Statutory changes to conditions of employment, inclusive of Pension, Provident and Medical Aid amendments;

5.3.2.2 Variations to hours of work and place of work after notification to the employee;

5.3.2.3 Changes to work methods, the re-organization and re-structuring of work, with notification to the employee;

5.3.2.4 Change to the performance of duties, related to the employee's core job functions and KPA's;

5.3.2.5 Variations in the event of remote and/or hybrid work practices as a result of changed work methods.

5.3.3 The employee agrees that the variations of contract in accordance with the provisions of this clause will not constitute breach of contract.

5.4 **Company Property**

5.4.1 All tools, equipment, goods, materials, parts and or component, machinery and vehicles supplied by the Company shall remain the property of the Company and must be treated as such.

5.4.2 Such property must be treated properly and cared for, and the employee is individually and jointly responsible for any equipment and or property issued to him. The employee will be liable for the intentional and/or negligent damage or loss or theft of Company property.

5.4.3 On termination of the employee's employment, the employee will immediately return to the Company all of the Company's property or any material relating to the affairs and business of the Company.

5.4.4 The employee unconditionally gives the personal assurance that no such items or copies of documents shall remain in his position.

5.5 **Security**

5.5.1 Notwithstanding the provisions of clauses 6.3.3, 6.3.4 and 6.3.5 of this contract, the Company's security regulations must be observed at all times, and may in the Company's sole discretion, be varied from time to time.

5.5.2 The employee may not unlawfully possess any substance, article or object that is the property of the Company, a client, or the property of any employee of the Company or client.

5.5.3 The employee shall be responsible for the safe custody, economical and effective utilization of any material, equipment or other property of the Company under the employee's supervision and control and shall report any damage thereto and or loss or theft thereof as soon as possible to the person under whose immediate authority duties are performed.

5.6 **Social Decorum**

The employee shall at all times be required to comply with social decorum which shall mean as follows –

5.6.1 An acceptable standard of social conduct at formal and or informal social gatherings with members of the public and/or clients and/or Company employees and/or Company representatives albeit it on or off the Company premises.

5.6.2 Such acceptable social conduct or decorum shall demand that all or any Company employee conduct shall be in such a manner as to not cause offence, affront, embarrassment or disorderliness in any matter by whatever means, irrespective of whether the Company acts as the host at such an event or not.

5.6.3 A serious breach hereof may warrant dismissal.

6. TERMINATION OF EMPLOYMENT/BREACH OF CONTRACT

6.1 This contract of employment may be terminated by way of written notice by either party as follows –

6.1.1 1 (one) week, if the employee has been employed for 6 (six) months or less;

6.1.2 2 (two) weeks, if the employee has been employed for more than 6 months but not more than 1 (one) year; and

6.1.3 4 (four) weeks, if the employee has been employed for 1 (one) year or more.

6.2 Unless agreed to the contrary between the parties –

6.2.1 Should the employee give notice and not tender his service during the notice period, the Company is entitled to recover the untenured portion in money from the employee; and

6.2.2 Should the Company choose not to let the employee tender services, then the Company will pay the employee in lieu of notice.

6.3 The following will constitute instances of material breach of contract and the employee will be liable for summary dismissal:

6.3.1 Poor work performance, defiance, rejection of control and authority, theft, assault, provocation, intimidation, absence without leave, incompetence, gross negligence, insubordination, disrespect, intoxication, dishonesty, disregard of safety rules, harassment, discrimination, social media abuse, damage to goods and/or property, deceitful conduct, unprocedural strike action, as well as conduct that results in the breakdown of the employment relationship.

7. RETIREMENT AGE

7.1 The parties specifically agree that the normal retirement age is at _____ years of age. The employee's service shall for this reason automatically expire at the end of the year in which he reaches the agreed retirement age.

7.2 The employee's retirement, having reached the mandatory retirement age of ___ , will constitute a termination by operation of law, and the same will not constitute a dismissal. The Company has a discretion to allow the employee to work beyond the age of ____ .

8. **AGREEMENT**

8.1 The employee warrants that he is not suffering from any medical defect, disability and/or ailment which will be an impairment for carrying out obligations in terms of this contract. Should the employee be in breach of this warranty, the Company shall have the option to terminate employment forthwith.

8.2 The failure of the employee to produce employment documentation such as security clearances, an identity document and/or passport, work permit documentation, educational certificates and/or proof of trade qualifications, upon request of the Company, could also result in the termination of this contract. In addition, this contract could be considered void *ab initio*, as a result.

Thus done and signed at ________________ on this ____ day of __________ 20__.

As a witness:	For and on behalf of **the Company** by
______________________________	______________________________

Thus done and signed at ________________ on this ____ day of __________ 20__.

As a witness:	The **employee**
______________________________	______________________________

SAMPLE
LETTER OF APPOINTMENT (STAFF/MANAGERIAL)

To: ____ Name of appointed employee

Dear ____________________,

Subject: LETTER OF APPOINTMENT

We have pleasure in confirming our offer of employment with ________ *("the Company")* on the terms and conditions set out hereunder. Please sign the enclosed duplicate copy of this letter indicating your acceptance and return this copy to the Company. The said terms and conditions constitute your contract of employment with the Company *("Contract of Employment").*

1. **COMMENCEMENT DATE**

1.1 You will commence your employment with the Company on ____________.

1.2 Employment with the Company will endure or an indefinite period whilst employed, unless terminated in accordance with the provisions relating to termination below.

2. **APPOINTMENT**

2.1 Your duties will be that of ____________________ (Job Title) (as outlined in Annexure A hereto).

2.2 You will report directly to ____________________.

2.3 You are required to perform your duties at ____________________ (physical address).

2.4 Your working hours are: Monday to Friday 08:30hrs to 17:00hrs with a half hour lunch break each day. Flexi hours are encouraged within reason.

2.5 From time to time you may be expected to perform your duties outside the stipulated hours of work.

2.6 In order to achieve optimal business performance and excellence, inclusive of the achievement of targets, you agree to accept and to adapt to changes in working conditions with the appropriate degree of flexibility.

3. **REMUNERATION AND SUBSTANTIVE CONDITIONS OF EMPLOYMENT**

3.1 Please refer to Annexure B which sets out your remuneration and conditions of employment package, basically in accordance with the provisions of the Basic Conditions of Employment Act *("BCEA").*

3.2 The Company reserves the right to review your salary once per annum. However, the Company does not guarantee increases. Increases are based on individual and Company performance and at the discretion of the Company. Individual performance may be measured in accordance with applicable Company Performance Management and Assessment Guidelines.

3.3 Accordingly, an annual bonus is not guaranteed and is at the entire discretion of the Company.

3.4 Change of occupation or change in rate of remuneration for the duration of this Agreement shall in no way alter any of the terms and conditions of this Agreement.

3.5 Your conditions of employment are primarily regulated by the applicable provisions of the BCEA, as amended, and in accordance with the terms and provisions of this Agreement.

3.6 As per Section 6(3) of the BCEA you are excluded from the following provisions as a result of earning more than the threshold provided for:

3.6.1 Section 9 (hours of work)

3.6.2 Section 10 (overtime)

3.6.3 Section 11 (working week)

3.6.4 Section 12 (average hours of work)

3.6.5 Section 14 (meal intervals)

3.6.6 Section 15 (daily and weekly rest periods)

3.6.7 Section 17 (2) (night work)

3.6.8 Section 18 (3) (public holidays)

The above provisions do not apply in the employment relationship and you do not automatically qualify to be paid overtime or for work performed outside of normal working hours. Arrangements in this regard in respect of remuneration or time off, will be by agreement.

4. IMPLIED WARRANTY OF SUITABILITY

4.1 You implicitly agree, promise and guarantee that:

4.1.1 you are competent to perform your contractual obligations and the work for which you were employed;

4.1.2 you will perform all functions and activities assigned to you to the best of your ability and in an efficient manner;

4.1.3 you will perform your duties in accordance with applicable Company policy, guidelines and instructions, custom and practice, as well as implied understandings;

4.1.4 you will meet performance and output targets as required;

4.1.5 underperformance or inability to achieve set standards could lead to the termination of your employment.

4.2 Your key performance areas and expected standards of output will be discussed with your immediate superior. Such key performance areas and standard of output form an integral part of this Agreement.

4.3 Both parties agree unconditionally that this Agreement is of a commercial nature based on mutual reciprocity and the economic and financial interests of both parties.

5. PROBATIONARY PERIOD (OPTIONAL)

5.1 The first 6 (six) months of your employment will be a probationary period which will run concurrently with the term of your contract and during which period either you or the Company will be entitled to terminate your employment on 1 (one) week's notice.

5.2 The probationary period constitutes a trial period and you agree that the Company will be entitled to terminate this Agreement in the event of incompatibility, poor work performance, and non-achievement of targets as well as in the event of misconduct.

5.3 With reference to paragraph 4 hereinabove, it is also agreed that the Company will be entitled to implement expedited consultations and performance improvement procedures, and where necessary, expedited termination procedures.

6. DEDUCTIONS FROM REMUNERATION

6.1 You agree to deductions from remuneration as follows:

▪ Reimbursement of personal, study medical or other loans; ▪ Salary in lieu of time not worked and/or services not provided; ▪ Failure to provide statutory or contractual notice period; ▪ Overpayments; ▪ Statutory deductions, UIF, PAYE and Workman's Compensation deductions	▪ Court/Garnishee orders; ▪ Loss or damage to property, or suffered as a result of theft or fraudulent conduct; ▪ Housing costs; ▪ Training costs; ▪ Meals/canteen facilities. ▪ Any other amount agreed to subject to section 34 of the BCEA

7. COMPANY RULES AND REGULATIONS

7.1 Schedule 8 to the Labour Relations Act – "A Code of Good Practice – Dismissal" will be applicable to the employment relationship, particularly in respect of misconduct, incapacity and ill health.

7.2 The Company's employment policies and procedures are provided under separate cover. In addition implied rules, as well as rules of custom and practice will apply.

7.3 Any grievances, problems or dissatisfactions which you may have must be raised with your immediate superior in the first instance.

7.4 You agree to submit to searches of person and possessions by persons designated by the Company, as and when necessary and at the discretion of management.

7.5 You warrant that, to the best of your knowledge, you are not suffering from any medical defect, disability or ailment which will impair the carrying out of his obligations in terms of this Agreement. Should you be in breach of this warranty, the Company shall have the option to terminate your employment forthwith.

7.6 You agree that when using the Company's electronic communications, such use must be in accordance with Company policies and that all electronic activities can and will be monitored and/or intercepted by the Company.

7.7 You further undertake to:

7.7.1 Obey and comply with all lawful and reasonable instructions, functions and duties as assigned to you

7.7.2 Be absolutely true and faithful to the Company in all dealings and transactions relating to the business and interests of the Company and to protect and promote the business, reputation and goodwill of the Company

7.7.3 Submit to management or any person nominated by management, such information and reports timeously as may be required in connection with the performance, duties and the business of the Company.

7.7.4 Devote the whole of your time and attention during the Company working hours, and such additional hours as are required to conduct the business affairs of the Company, inclusive of your duties.

8. CONFIDENTIALITY, RESTRICTIONS AND RESTRAINT OF TRADE

8.1 You are prohibited to supply any goods, information, or to render any services to any clients, competitors, their employees or representatives, suppliers or any employee of the Company except as may be required in the course of your employment.

8.2 In the course of your duties, you will be exposed to or privy to information of a personal, private or confidential nature relating to the Company and its products. All such information is proprietary in nature and is the exclusive property of the Company.

8.3 You are expressly and specifically forbidden to disclose such information to or discuss it with any person in the Company's employ or outside other than with your superior and immediate co-employees who are authorized to deal with these matters. You are further specifically prohibited from making use of any such information after your contract with the Company has been terminated

8.4 You are not entitled to receive any gifts, money and/or benefits from clients or prospective clients without the prior approval of the Company.

8.5 Inventions or other innovations may fall within the scope of your employment. Such inventions or other innovations are deemed to be the property of the Company and you will assign such inventions and innovations to the Company upon request. You will also sign any forms necessary in the protection of such inventions and other innovations in Southern African and elsewhere.

8.6 To avoid any conflict of interest, you agree not to engage directly and/or indirectly in any alternative employment whilst remaining in the Company's employ, without written permission of the Company. The specific intent of this Agreement is that you remain loyal to and act in the best interests of the Company and devote all your time, skills and knowledge in the interests of the Company.

8.7 You acknowledge that the Company has an extremely high degree of competition and that it is imperative that all such information, not published by the Company to the general public constitutes trade secrets, confidential and proprietary to the Company.

8.8 Accordingly you as well as every employee is required specifically not to disclose, during and following your employment, the production, marketing, professional and organizational secrets or other confidential information of the Company, its affiliated companies, or its customers to a competitor or third party.

8.9 This obligation shall remain in effect for as long as the confidential information remains a secret, or in any event, for a period of at least 6 (six) months from the date of termination of your service with the Company.

8.10 Breach of confidentiality could result in summary dismissal and/or legal action of whatsoever nature against yourself and/or associates. You are in agreement that the Company is entitled by law to pursue any claims against you and/or your associates at the time in the event of alleged breaches of confidentiality and/or restraint of trade, in order to protect the interests of the Company.

9. **COMPANY PROPERTY**

9.1 All vehicles, equipment and goods supplied by the Company shall remain the property of the Company and must be cared for accordingly.
9.2 Such Company's property is to be cared for and you are individually and jointly responsible for any equipment or property issued to yourself. You will be liable for the intentional and/or negligent damage or loss of Company property.
9.3 On termination of your employment, you will immediately return to the Company all of the Company's property or any material relating to the affairs and business of the Company.
9.4 You unconditionally give the personal assurance that no such items/ copies of documents will remain in your possessions.
9.5 Corporate information is generated, obtained and contained by various methods, e.g., verbal communication, documentation, internet, email, telephone, social media, cell phone and computers. This corporate information is for the sole benefit of the Company.
9.6 You fully recognize and acknowledge that the Company has intellectual property assets and has established measures and assigned responsibilities to protect those assets from abuse, loss, theft, unauthorized modification and disclosure.
9.7 In order to protect the Company's corporate information and intellectual property and assets, the Company reserves the right, (and you unconditionally authorize the Company thereto) to monitor electronic communications and/or to intercept email transmissions, internet usage, computer utilization, telephone conversations, and social media, as may be required to protect the Company's interests.

10. **SECURITY**

10.1 The Company's security regulations must be observed at all times, and may in the Company's sole discretion, be varied from time to time.
10.2 You may not unlawfully possess any substance, article or object that is the property of the Company, or the property of any employee of the Company.

10.3 You shall be responsible for the safe custody and economical and effective utilization of any material, equipment or other property of the Company under your supervision and control, and shall report any damage thereto or loss thereof as soon as possible to the person under whose immediate authority you perform your duties.

10.4 The Company shall be entitled, at its discretion, but in accordance with due process to require you to subject yourself to:

10.4.1 Medical examination and/or medical treatment and/or medical testing within the confines of law;

10.4.2 Alcohol, drug and/or illegal substance testing;

10.4.3 Polygraph testing;

10.4.4 Security clearances.

11. SOCIAL DECORUM

11.1 You shall at all times be required to comply with social decorum which shall mean:

11.1.1 An acceptable standard of social conduct at formal and/or informal social gatherings with members of the public and/or customers and/or Company Employees and/or representatives albeit it on or off Company premises;

11.1.2 Such social conduct/decorum shall demand that all or any Company employee conduct himself/herself in such a manner as not to cause offence, affront, embarrassment or disorderliness in any manner by whatever means irrespective of whether the Company acts as the host at such an event or not.

11.1.3 A serious breach hereof may warrant dismissal.

12. DOCUMENTATION

12.1 On your starting date, you must have the following certified documents available, and must ensure that they are correct. If during your employment with the Company any of the personal information as supplied below should change then you must inform the Company within 30 (thirty) days of such changes:

12.1.1 Proof of highest academic qualification;

12.1.2 Identity document;

12.1.3 Tax reference number;

12.1.4 Banking details;

12.1.5 Any other personal information (marriage certificate, spouse's identity document, birth certificates of children, etc.);

12.1.6 Driver's license;

12.1.7 Other documentation and/or certification at the discretion of the Company.

12.1 Any false information or withholding of information on your part, which may have influenced the appointment, may lead to this Agreement being summarily terminated.

13. VARIATIONS AND CHANGES

13.1 With the exception of the variations of contract provided for in clauses 2.6 and 13.2 hereof, no provision of this contract may be amended, substituted or otherwise varied, and no provision may be added to or incorporated in this contract, except by an agreement in writing between you and the Company.

13.2 You agree and consent to the following variations and changes that be effected by the Company dependent on circumstances:

13.2.1 Statutory changes to conditions of employment, inclusive of Pension, Provident and Medical Aid amendments;

13.2.2 Changes in respect of hours and place of work, after notification to yourself;

13.2.3 Work methods and the re-organization and re-structuring of work, with notification to yourself;

13.2.4 Variations in respect of the performance of additional duties, related to your core job functions and KPA's;

13.2.5 Changes that may be necessary in the event of remote and/or hybrid work practices, in order to optimize Company performance and excellence;

14. TERMINATION OF EMPLOYMENT/NOTICE PERIOD

14.1 Notice of termination of employment must be given in writing by either party. The notice of termination may not be given nor run concurrently with any period of leave.

14.2 You will be subject to the relevant notice periods in terms of the BCEA. These notice periods are as follows:

14.2.1 1 (one) week's written notice, if you have been employed for 6 (six) months or less;

14.2.2 2 (two) week's written notice, if you have been employed for more than 6 (six) months but not more than 1 (one) year;

14.2.3 4 (four) week's written notice, if you have been employed for 1 (one) year or more.

14.3 Unless otherwise agreed to between the parties:

14.3.1 Should you give notice and not tender service during the notice period, the Company will be entitled to recover the untenured portion in money from yourself;

14.3.2 Should the Company choose not to let you tender your services, the Company must pay you in lieu of notice;

14.4 Despite the foregoing, either party may terminate the contract without notice for any cause recognized in law as sufficient to warrant summary dismissal. The following will constitute material breach of contract:

14.4.1 Dishonesty, theft, fraud and/or falsification, assault, provocation, intimidation, absence without leave, gross incompetence, gross negligence, insubordination and disrespect, intoxication, disregard of safety rules, damage to goods and/or property, or unauthorized possession of goods, incompatibility, breach of confidentiality, information technology and internet abuse and conduct which could lead to the destruction of the employment trust relationship;

14.4.2 Schedule 8 to the Labour Relations Act, "A Code of Good Practice: Dismissal" is also generally applicable to the terms and conditions of this agreement.

15. RETIREMENT AGE

15.1 The parties specifically agree that the normal retirement age is at ____ years of age. Your service shall for this reason automatically terminate at the end of the year in which you reach the agreed retirement age, and the same will not constitute a dismissal but a termination in law.

16. FORCE MAJEURE

16.1 Neither you or the Company will be liable for the delay or failure to perform any obligation and or undertaking in terms of this contract in the event and to the extent that such delay or failure is caused by force majeure including but not limited to an act of God, fire, lightening, earthquake, explosion, flood, emergency, insurrection, civil disorder, war, military operations, pandemic, act of terrorism or the declaration of a state of emergency or national disaster.

17. **GENERAL**

17.1 By signing this Letter of Appointment inclusive of Annexure A and B thereto, you accept employment with the Company and in particular confirm that you have been made aware of, and fully understand the contents of this Agreement, inclusive of the terms and employment conditions offered by the Company.

17.2 You specifically undertake to be legally bound by this Agreement and to abide by its provisions.

We are very pleased to welcome you to the Company and are confident that you will enjoy the opportunity and rise to the challenge. If you have any queries regarding your employment or on any other associated matter, please do not hesitate to discuss same.

Signed in ______________________ on the ______ day of ________________ 20__.

Signed: **COMPANY** ______________________	Date ______________________
Signed: **EMPLOYEE** ______________________	Date ______________________

EXAMPLE

ANNEXURE A

POSITION: ____________________

DEPARTMENT: ____________________

LOCATION: ____________________

Organizational Fit	**Purpose of Role**
Reports: ____________ Director Reports/ Subordinates____________ Peers:____________	e.g. To achieve and to maintain the following ____________

Accountabilities & Responsibilities/Key Performance Areas	
Accountabilities: (LIST)	
Responsibilities: (LIST)	**Key Activities: (LIST)**
e.g. Achievement of ____________	▪ Setting and allocation of business objectives ▪ Input into and execution of ____________ ▪ Budget planning and cost management ▪ Key performance activities not limited to but including ____________
Business planning and performance management	▪ e.g. Business analysis and planning, including development of the business plan & co-ordination of the planning process; customer segmentation & targeting activities; and appropriate resource allocation. ▪ Setting business objectives; tracking performance & taking appropriate action. ▪ Development of market & competitor knowledge. ▪ Build appropriate business relationships; developing and leverage relationships and act as the Company representative. ▪ Fellow management ▪ In conjunction with ______; set appropriate objectives; co-ordinate roles & responsibilities; ensure effective team communication & meetings. ▪ Interactive & communication with and with other internal Company functions.

<table>
<tr><td>Market knowledge and customer development</td><td>▪ Development of market & competitor knowledge
▪ Build appropriate business relationships; develop and leverage relationships and act as the Company representative
▪ Fellow management</td></tr>
<tr><td>Team leadership & management</td><td>▪ In conjunction with _______; set appropriate objectives; co-ordinate roles and responsibilities; ensure effective team communication & meetings.
▪ Interaction & communication with and with other internal Company functions.</td></tr>
<tr><td>Team development & coaching</td><td>▪ Performance input into appraisal & regular performance feedback
▪ Regular 1:1 representative interactions</td></tr>
<tr><td>Implementation of marketing strategies</td><td>▪ Implementation of global strategies into the local market.</td></tr>
<tr><td colspan="2">Authority & Quantitative Dimensions

▪ People: Manage
▪ Products: Responsible for all products</td></tr>
<tr><td colspan="2">Primary Working Relationships

▪ Internally: ______________________________
▪ Externally: ______________________________</td></tr>
<tr><td colspan="2">Specific Demands & Environment Factors, e.g.:

▪ Regular travel; frequent overnight stays
▪ Flexible working hours to meet deadlines and meetings being held.</td></tr>
</table>

ANNEXURE B

REMUNERATION AND CONDITIONS OF EMPLOYMENT PACKAGE (GROSS)

NAME: ______________________ **POSITION:** ______________________

		PER MONTH	PER ANNUM
1.	**SALARY**	R ____________	R ____________
2.	**13TH CHEQUE**	R ____________	
3.	**PERFORMANCE BONUS**	Up to _____ % of Annual Salary	
	3.1 Based on predetermined performance criteria 3.2 Other e.g. incentives, achievements of targets		
4.	**MOTOR ALLOWANCE**	R ____________	R ____________
	4.1 Self insurance 4.2 Petrol PD by Company (all work related mileage) 4.3 Maintenance paid @ R ___ per/km work related		
5.	**PROVIDENT FUND** Payable by Employer	____ % of Basic Taxable Salary	

6. **MEDICAL AID**

Company will pay an amount of R____ per month for your ____ Medical Plan for 1 member and 2 dependents

7. **CELL PHONE**

Company to provide a phone. All business calls will be covered by the Company

8. **LEAVE**

8.1 **Annual Leave**

8.1.1 You are entitled to 21 (twenty-one) working days leave on full pay in respect of each period of 12 consecutive months of service.

8.1.2 Leave accrues at the rate of 1.67 days for each completed month of service.

8.1.3 At the Company's discretion you may be required to take leave between Christmas and New Year.

8.1.4 Not more than 3 (three) weeks continuous annual leave may be taken.

8.2 **Sick Leave and Absenteeism**

8.2.1 You are entitled to 30 (thirty) days sick leave over a period of 36 (thirty-six) consecutive months. During the first 6 (six) months of employment you are entitled to 1 (one) day's sick leave for every completed month of service

8.2.1 You are required to notify your immediate superior in advance or on the morning of the first day, or as soon as reasonably possible, or any illness.

8.2.1 You agree that should you be booked off sick you shall provide the Company with a medical certificate from a registered medical practitioner.

8.2.1 Should you be off sick on a Monday and/or Friday, you agree to provide a medical certificate from a registered medical practitioner.

8.2.1 Any employee who is absent without authorized leave or without contacting management for a period exceeding 2 (two) consecutive days, on a Monday, Friday day before or after a public holiday, will be in breach of contract and may be liable for disciplinary action and/or summary dismissal.

8.2.1 During the period of your contract of employment, you will be entitled to 1 (one) day's sick leave for every 26 (twenty-six) days worked, accumulative to a maximum of 36 (thirty-six) days over a period of 3 (three) years.

8.3 **Maternity and Paternity Leave**
See Statutory entitlements/policy

8.1 **Public Holidays**
As per Statute

9. **RETIREMENT FUND** (If applicable Company details)

10. **OTHER** (Refer to additional policies and procedures, if applicable)

SAMPLE

LIMITED DURATION/TEMPORARY OR PROJECT BASED

CONTRACT OF EMPLOYMENT

MADE AND ENTERED INTO BY AND BETWEEN

______________________________	______________________________
(name of Employer)	(with address at)

Herein represented by ____ duly authorized hereto (hereinafter referred to as the *"Employer")*

AND

______________________________	______________________________
(name of Employee)	(with address at)

______________________________	______________________________
(identity number)	(mobile number)

(hereinafter referred to as the *"Employee")*

For further purposes of this agreement, the male shall import the female and vice versa, and reference to "company" shall include reference to "employer".

WHEREAS

1.1 The Company appoints the employee to provide services and the employee accepts such appointment by the Company.

1.2 The employee is able to provide the services required by the Company and warrants that he is suitably organized, qualified and experienced in the provision of the services referred to and required in terms of this contract.

1.3 The parties hereto wish to record and reduce this agreement into writing, in order to constitute a written contract of employment.

WHEREBY THE PARTIES AGREE AS FOLLOWS:

1. **INTRODUCTION**

    1.1 The Company has offered employment to the employee on a temporary, fixed term basis. The contract will therefore automatically expire on any of the events provided for in clause 3 hereof.

1.2 Both parties agree unconditionally that this contract is of a commercial nature based on mutual reciprocity and the economic, business and financial interests of both parties. Should it become apparent to either party that there is no mutual financial and or other benefit that results from this contract then either party will be entitled to terminate this contract in accordance with the provisions contained herein.

1.3 The Company appoints the employee in a temporary capacity to provide the agreed services, and the employee accepts such appointment by the Company.

1.4 The employee is able to provide the services required by the Company and warrants that he is suitably organized, qualified, and experienced in the provision of the services referred to and required in terms of this contract.

2. APPOINTMENT, DUTIES AND GUARANTEES

2.1 It is hereby confirmed that the employee has been offered and has accepted temporary employment with the Company as a ____________________ (job title) of ____________________ (premises/site)

2.2 The Company hereby appoints the employee to provide the following core services:

2.2.1 ____

2.2.2 ____

2.2.3 ____

2.2.4 ____

2.3 In order to achieve Company objectives and individual targets, the employee unconditionally confirms, recognizes and supports the complete flexibility of the tasks and duties which he was appointed for and must comply with all instructions, inclusive of the performance of additional duties and tasks as and when required by the Company. By accepting this offer of employment you agree that you will be flexible in accepting and adapting to change in your working conditions.

2.4 With due regard to the provisions of section 198B(3) and (4) of the LRA, the employee agrees that this contract is of a limited duration and that he can have no expectations of a renewal and or extension of this temporary contract of employment.

2.5 The employee implicitly agrees ad promises that –

2.5.1 He is competent to perform contractual obligations and the work employed for;

2.5.1 He will perform all functions and activities assigned to the best of his ability and in an efficient manner;

2.5.1 He will perform duties in accordance with Company policy, guidelines and instructions, custom and practice, as well as implied understandings;

2.5.1 He guarantees that agreed performance and output targets required by the Company will be met and achieved. The employee further agrees that underperformance, inclusive of inefficiency and incompetence, or the inability to achieve set standards, could lead to dismissal.

3. DURATION

3.1 This agreement will continue until it automatically terminates on the earliest of any of the following dates or events –

(a) on ____________________ (date); or

(b) upon completion of the following project: _______________ (name and project) with estimated completion time of ___________ months/years; or

(c) upon the completion of the purpose or tasks(s) for which the employee was appointed; or

(d) Upon the Company's client cancelling the project/contract/assignment at any given stage.

4. REMUNERATION AND CONDITIONS OF EMPLOYMENT

4.1 The employee shall be paid a monthly/weekly salary of R_______________ (state amount) payable by EFT/cash (delete as applicable).

4.2 Deductions:

4.2.1 The employee unconditionally agrees to deductions from remuneration to be made by the Company:

▪ Reimbursement of personal, study medical or other loans; ▪ Salary in lieu of time not worked and/or services not provided; ▪ Failure to provide statutory or contractual notice period; ▪ Overpayments; ▪ Statutory deductions, UIF, PAYE and Workman's Compensation deductions;	▪ Court/Garnishee orders; ▪ Loss or damage to property, or suffered as a result of theft or fraudulent conduct; ▪ Housing costs; ▪ Training costs; ▪ Meals/canteen facilities; ▪ Any other amount agreed to but subject to section 34 of the BCEA.

4.3 Conditions of employment is regulated by the provisions of the Basic Conditions of Employment Act (or any applicable Wage Determination, Bargaining Council Agreement or Sectoral Determination).

4.4 Short-term, temporary employment conditions are as follows:

4.4.1 **Hours of work**

The employee's weekly hours of work shall be –

(a) From Monday to Friday _________ (from) _________ (to); or

(b) In accordance with a weekly/fortnightly/monthly work/shift schedule

(provided that in both cases (a) and (b), ordinary working hours will not exceed 45 hours per week.)

4.4.2 **Meal & Other Intervals**

The employee is entitled to a meal interval of 30 minutes, which does not form part of normal working hours. The Employer, entirely at his discretion, may make allowance for other intervals, which would be considered part of normal working hours.

4.4.3 **Overtime**

The employee agrees to work overtime, on Sundays or public holidays, when required, at prevailing overtime rates.

4.4.4 **Sick Leave**

4.4.4.1 During the first 6 (six) months of employment, the employee is entitled to 1 (one) day's paid sick leave for every 26 (twenty-six) days worked. After a period of 6 (six) months, the employee will be entitled to 30 (thirty) days sick leave over a sick leave cycle of 36 (thirty-six) months.

4.4.4.2 Should the employee be unable to attend work because of illness, the employee is required to notify his manager before 10h00 on that day.

4.4.4.3 The Employer is not required to pay the employee sick leave in the event of:

4.4.4.4 The employee being absent from work for more than 2 (two) consecutive days; and/or

4.4.4.5 The employee being absent from work more than 2 (two) occasions during an 8 (eight) week period; and/or

4.4.4.6 On request by the Employer, failure by the employee to produce a medical certificate stating that he was unable to work for the duration of his absence on account of sickness or injury; and/or

4.4.4.7 The employee abusing sick leave provisions.

4.4.5 **Maternity/Paternity Leave**

Due to the brief duration of this agreement, the legislative entitlements pertaining to maternity/paternity leave will provisionally not apply.

4.4.6 **Annual Leave**

Should the duration of this agreement be for a period of 4 months or longer, the employee shall be entitled to one day's leave per 17 days worked, or if paid hourly, one hour's leave per 17 hours worked. Leave may only be taken at a time to be agreed or as determined by the Employer.

4.4.7 **Family Responsibility Leave**

If the duration of this agreement is for a period of 4 months or longer, and the employee does not work for less than 4 days a week, the employee is entitled to conditional family responsibility leave in terms of section27(2) of the BCEA.

5. SHORT TIME

5.1. Should the employer be unable to productively employ the employee for the ordinary hours of work per week due to slackness of trade, shortage of raw materials, a general breakdown of plant or machinery caused by an accident or any other unforeseen emergency, the employer may implement short time during, but not exceeding the period of unforeseen circumstances. For a period of short time the employee will be remunerated for the hours worked. Where practically possible, written notice regarding the implementation of short time must be given to the employee in writing at least 24 hours prior to, or less if the circumstances are more urgent of the date of which short time will be implemented.

6. HEALTH AND SAFETY

6.1 The employee undertakes not to be in breach of safety and health rules and regulations. Both parties acknowledge that the obligation to ensure that the workplace is a safe and healthy environment conducive to maximal performance and productivity rests primarily on the Employer.

6.2 The duties and general duty of care referred to hereinabove is applicable to on, as well as off, Company premises, and are equally applicable to hybrid, remote and work-from-home practices. The employee agrees to be cooperative in response to the Employer's health and safety measures and will not be obstructive in respect of health and safety instructions and/or directives.

6.3 Statutory Regulations as well as Company rules and guidelines in respect of the safety and health of employees and the population at large, must be taken into consideration in order to achieve and to further enhance a safe and healthy work environment. Disregard for such rules and regulations could lead to discipline and dismissal.

7. COMPANY RULES AND REGULATIONS

7.1 Schedule 8 to the Labour Relationship Act: "A Code of Good Conduct – Dismissal" is applicable as a Guideline Code to this agreement in respect of:

7.1.1 Disciplinary measures;
7.1.2 Dismissal;
7.1.3 Probation (if applicable);
7.1.4 Poor Work Performance;
7.1.5 Incapacity and ill-health;
7.1.6 Medical incapacity.

7.2 Company rules of conduct, employment policies and procedures are available separately from Company Management.

7.2.1 The employee agrees that it is necessary for the Employer to implement measures and procedures on an on-going basis, in order to protect and to further the Employer's business, as well as the safety, health and wellbeing of fellow employees and customers. The employee further agrees to and gives his irrevocable consent to any examination and/or testing for such purpose, including, but not limited to:

7.2.1.1 Medical examinations and/or testing, excluding testing prohibited by law;
7.2.1.2 Blood, urine or breathalyser/alcohol tests;
7.2.1.3 Drug and or any illegal substance testing;
7.2.1.4 Polygraph testing;
7.2.1.5 Fingerprint examination and/or security clearances.

7.2.2 The employee agrees to searching of his person or property in the event of a reasonable suspicion of misconduct and/or as part of access control measures to the premises of the employer.

7.2.3 The employee is aware of, agrees and consents to the monitoring of any premises and/or vehicles from where the employee may be conducting work and duties, by means of electronic surveillance and/or surveillance equipment and/or similar equipment, provided that such surveillance complies with statutory requirements.

8. TERMINATION OF EMPLOYMENT/BREACH OF CONTRACT

8.1 During its existence and irrespective of clause 3 hereinabove, the contract of employment may be terminated by way of written notice by either party as follows -

8.1.1 1 (one) week, if the employee has been employed for 6 (six) months or less;

8.1.2 2 (two) weeks, if the employee has been employed for more than 6 months but not more than 1 (one) year; and

8.1.3 4 (four) weeks, if the employee has been employed for 1 (one) year or more; and

8.1.4 Should the employee resign in breach of clause 3 hereof the Employer reserves the right to recover damages from the employee.

8.2 Unless otherwise agreed to between the parties -

8.2.1 Should the employee give notice and not tender his service during the notice period, the Employer is entitled to recover the untenured portion in money from the employee; and

8.2.2 Should the Employer choose not to let the employee tender services, then the Employer will pay the employee in lieu of notice.

8.3 The employee will be liable for summary dismissal in the following instances:

8.3.1 Poor work performance, defiance, rejection of control of authority, theft, assault, sabotage, provocation, intimidation, absence without leave, incompetence, gross negligence, insubordination and disrespect, intoxication, dishonesty, disregard of safety rules, damage to goods and or property, deceitful conduct, refusal to carry out instructions, unprocedural strike action, and any conduct that results in the breakdown of the employment relationship.

9. AGREEMENT

9.1 The employee warrants that he is not suffering from any medical defect, disability and or ailment which will impair him from carrying out of his obligations in terms of this contract. Should the employee be in breach of this warranty the Employer shall have the option to terminate employment forthwith.

9.2 The failure of the employee to produce employment documentation such as security clearances, an identity document and/or passport, work permit documentation, educational certificates and/or proof of trade qualifications, upon request of the Employer, could also result in the termination of this contract. In addition, this contract could be considered void *ab initio,* as a result.

10. FORCE MAJEURE

Neither party will be liable for the delay or failure to perform any obligation and or undertaking in terms of this contract in the event and to the extent that such delay or failure is caused by force majeure including but not limited to an act of God, fire, lightening, earthquake, explosion, flood, emergency, insurrection, civil disorder, war, military operations, pandemic, act of terrorism or the declaration of a state of emergency or national disaster.

Thus done and signed at __________________ on this ____ day of __________ 20__.

As a witness:	For and on behalf of **the Employer** by
____________________	____________________ Who warrants authority hereto

Thus done and signed at __________________ on this ____ day of __________ 20__.

As a witness:	The **employee**
____________________	____________________

SAMPLE

DOMESTIC WORKER'S CONTRACT OF EMPLOYMENT

(DEPARTMENT OF LABOUR)

Given by:

____

(herein after referred to as "the employer")

Address of employer:	....
	....
	....
	....

to

____

(herein after referred to as "the employee")

1. **Commencement**
   Employment will begin on .... and continue until terminated as set out in clause 6 of the guidelines.

2. **Place of work** ....

3. **Job description** ....

   Job Title ....
   (e.g.. Domestic worker, child minder, gardener, etc)

   Duties: See attached job description

4. **Hours of work** *(See Guideline 5)*
   4.1 Normal working hours will be .... hours per week, made up as follows:
   Monday/Tuesday/Wednesday/Thursday/Friday: .... am to .... pm
   Meal intervals will be from: .... to ....
   Other breaks: ....
   Saturdays: .... am to .... pm
   Meal intervals will be from: .... to ....
   Other breaks: ....
   Sundays: .... am to .... pm
   Meal intervals will be from: .... to ....

Other breaks: ....

4.2 Overtime will only be worked as agreed from time to time and will be paid at the rate of one and a half times of the total wage as set out in clause 5.2.

4.3 Standby will only be done if agreed from time to time whereby an allowance will be paid of at least R20,00 per standby shift.

5. **Wage** *(See Guidelines 4 and 5)*

5.1	The employees wage shall be paid in cash on the last working day of every week/month and shall be:	R.............
5.2	The employee shall be entitled to the following allowances/other cash payments/payment in kind:	
5.2.1	A weekly/monthly transport allowance of	R.............
5.2.2	Accommodation per week/month to the value of	R.............
5.3	The following deductions are agreed upon:	R..............
	....	R..............
	....	R..............
	....	R..............
5.4	The total value of the above remuneration shall be *(The total of clauses 5.1 to 5.2.2)* *(Modify or delete clauses 5.2.1 to 5.2.2 as needed)*	R................
5.5	The employer shall review the employee's salary/wage on or before 1 November of every year.	

6. **Termination of employment**

Either party can terminate this agreement with one weeks notice during the first six months of employment and with four weeks notice thereafter. Notice must be given in writing except when it is given by an illiterate domestic worker. In the case where the domestic worker is illiterate notice must be explained orally by or on behalf of the employer.

7. **Sunday work**

Any work on Sundays will be by agreement between parties and will be paid according to clause 7 of the guidelines.

8. **Public Holidays**

Any work on holidays will be by agreement and will be paid according to clause 8 of the guidelines.

9. **Annual Leave**

The employee is entitled to three weeks paid leave after every 12 months of continuous service. Such leave is to be taken at times convenient to the employer and the employer may require the employee to take his/her leave at such times as coincide with that of the employer.

10. **Sick leave**

10.1 During every sick leave cycle of 36 months the employee will be entitled to an amount of paid sick leave equal to the number of days the employee would normally work during a period of six weeks.
10.2 During the first six months of employment the employee will entitled to one day's paid sick leave for every 26 days worked.
10.3 The employee is to notify the employer as soon as possible in case of his/her absence from work through illness.
10.4 A medical certificate may be required if absent for more than 2 consecutive days or has been absent on more than two occasions during an eight-week period.

11. **Maternity leave**
(Tick the applicable clauses in the space provided).

11.1	The employee will be entitled to .... months maternity leave without pay; or	☐
11.2	The employee will be entitled to .... months maternity leave on .... pay	☐

12. **Family responsibility leave**

The employee will be entitled to five days family responsibility leave during each leave cycle if he or she works on at least four days a week.

13. **Accommodation**
(Tick the applicable boxes).

14.1	The employee will be provided with accommodation for as long as the employee is in the service of the employer, which shall form part of his/her remuneration package.	☐
14.2	The accommodation may only be occupied by the worker, unless prior arrangement with the employer.	☐
14.3	Prior permission should be obtained for visitors who wish to stay the night. However where members of the employees direct family are visiting, such permission will not be necessary.	☐

14. **Clothing *(Delete this clause if not applicable)***

.... sets of uniforms will be supplied to the employee free of charge by the employer and will remain the property of the employer.

15. **Other conditions of employment or benefits**

....

....

....

....

....

16. **General**

Any changes to the written particulars will only be valid if agreed to by both parties.

....

EMPLOYER

Acknowledgement of receipt by employee:

....

Date: ....

JOB DESCRIPTION

Indicate functions required by a 4 in the appropriate block

Child minding/baby sitting	☐	Laundry – machine wash	☐
Minding old/sick employer or relative	☐	Laundry – hand wash	☐
General tidying of house	☐	Hanging out of laundry	☐
Making of beds	☐	Washing of curtains	☐
Vacuuming of carpets	☐	Ironing	☐
Vacuuming of upholstery	☐	Small mending job, e.g. replacing buttons, hems, etc	☐
Dusting	☐	Defrosting and cleaning fridge & freezer	☐
Wiping down of all appliances e.g. T.V etc	☐	Cleaning of windows and glass doors inside and out	☐
Cleaning of walls, light switches, doors etc	☐	Cleaning of all used equipment e.g. vacuum cleaner	☐
Cleaning of ornaments	☐	Packing away of groceries	☐
Cleaning of toilets, basins, baths, showers, taps etc.	☐	Removal of refuse for collection	☐
Mopping of tiled/vinyl floors	☐	Sweeping of outside patios, steps, etc	☐
Cleaning of inside of cupboards	☐	Wiping down of outside lights	☐
Cleaning of stove and oven	☐	Cleaning of outside rooms and cloakroom	☐
Preparation/cooking of breakfast	☐	General driving duties and errands	☐
Preparation/cooking of lunch	☐	Wash cars	☐
Preparation/cooking of supper	☐	Maintain garden in clean and tidy condition	☐
Setting of table	☐	Caring for pool	☐
Cleaning away after breakfast/lunch/supper	☐	Mow lawns	☐
Polishing of floors and verandas	☐	Weeding	☐
Cleaning brass and silver	☐	Trimming and pruning	☐
Washing of Walls	☐	Washing and grooming of dogs	☐
Other...	☐	Painting of walls	☐
....	☐	....	☐

GUIDELINES

1. **Notice period and termination of employment**

In terms of the Sectoral Determination, any party to an employment contract must give written notice, except when an illiterate domestic worker gives it, as follows:

- One week, if employed for six months or less
- Four weeks if employed for more than six months.

Notice must be explained orally by or on behalf of the employer to a domestic worker if he/she is not able to understand it. The employer is required to provide the domestic worker who resides in accommodation that is situated on the premises of the employer or that is supplied by the employer, with accommodation for a period of one month, or if it is a longer period, until the contract of employment could lawfully have been terminated.

All monies due to the domestic worker for any wages, allowance or other payments that have not been paid, paid time-off not taken and pro-rata leave must be paid.

2. **Procedure for termination of employment**

Whilst the contract of employment makes provision for termination of employment, it must be understood that the services of an employee may not be terminated unless a valid and fair reason exists and fair procedure is followed. If an employee is dismissed without a valid reason or without a fair procedure, the employee may approach the CCMA for assistance.

Pro-rata leave and severance pay might be payable. In the event of a domestic worker being unable to return to work due to disability, the employer must investigate the nature of the disability and ascertain whether or not it is permanent or temporary. The employer must try to accommodate the employee as far as possible for example, amending or adapting their duties to suit the disability.

However, in the event of it not being possible for the employer to adapt the domestic workers duties and/or to find alternatives, then such employer may terminate the services of the domestic worker. The Labour Relations Act, 66 of 1995 sets out the procedures to be followed at the termination of services in the Code of Good Practice, in Schedule 8.

3. **Wage/Remuneration/Payment**

There is a prescribed minimum rate of remuneration. Additional payments (such as for overtime or work on Sundays or Public Holidays) are calculated from the total remuneration as indicated in clause 5.3 of the contract. The total remuneration is the total of the money received by the employee and the payment in kind, which may not be more than 10% of the wage for accommodation.

4. **Transport allowances**

Sectoral Determination 7: Domestic Sector, South Africa does not regulate this and is therefore open to negotiation between the parties.

5. **Hours of work**

5.1 Normal hours (excluding overtime)

A domestic worker may not be made to:

- work more than 45 hours a week;
- work more than nine hours per day for a five day work week;
- work more than eight hours a day for a six day work week; and

5.2 Overtime

A domestic worker may not work more than 15 hours overtime per week but may not work more than 12 hours on any day, including overtime. Overtime must be paid at 1.5 times the employee's normal wage or an employee may agree to receive paid time off.

5.3 Daily and weekly rest periods

5.3.1 A daily rest period of 12 consecutive hours and a weekly rest period of 36 consecutive hours, which must include Sunday, unless otherwise agreed, must be allowed.

5.3.2 The daily rest period may by agreement be reduced to 10 hours for an employee who live on the premises whose meal interval lasts for at least three hours.

5.3.3 The weekly rest period may by agreement be extended to 60 consecutive hours every two weeks or be reduced to eight hours in any week if the rest period in the following week is extended equivalently.

5.4 Standby

5.4.1 Standby means any period between 20:00 and 06:00 the next day when a domestic worker is required to be at the workplace and is permitted to rest or sleep but must be available to work if necessary.

5.4.2 May only done if it is agreed in writing and on not more than five times per month must be compensated by the payment of an allowance of at least R20,00 per shift.

5.5 Night work - after 18:00 and before 06:00

5.5.1 Worked only if agreed to in writing and must be compensated by an allowance and if the domestic resides at the workplace or transport is available.

6. **Meal intervals**

A domestic worker is entitled to a one-hour break for a meal after not more than five hours work. Such interval may be reduced to 30 minutes, by agreement between the parties. When a second meal interval is required because of overtime worked, it may be reduced to not less than 15 minutes. If required or permitted to work during this period, remuneration must be paid.

7. **Sunday work**

Work on Sundays is voluntary and a domestic worker can therefore not be forced to work on a Sunday. If the employee works on a Sunday he/she shall be paid double the daily wage. If the employee ordinarily works on a Sunday he/she shall be paid one and one-half time the wage for every hour worked. Paid time off in return for working on a Sunday may be agreed upon.

8. **Public Holidays**

The days mentioned in the Public Holidays Act must be granted but the parties can agree to further public holidays. Work on a public holiday is entirely voluntary and a domestic worker may not be forced to work on such public holiday.

The official public holidays are:

New Year's Day
Human Rights Day
Good Friday
Family Day
Freedom Day
Workers Day
Youth Day
National Woman's Day
Heritage Day
Day of Reconciliation
Christmas Day
Day of Goodwill

Any other day declared an official public holiday from time to time should also be granted. These days can be exchanged for any other day by agreement. If the employee works on a public holiday he/she shall be paid double the normal days wage.

9. **Annual Leave**

Annual leave may not be less than three weeks per year for full-time workers or by agreement, one day for every 17 days worked or one hour for every 17 hours worked. The leave must be granted not later than six months after completion of the period of 12 consecutive months of employment. The leave may not be granted concurrent with any period of sick leave, nor with a period of notice of termination of the contract of employment.

10. **Sick leave**

During every sick leave cycle of 36 months an employee is entitled to an amount of paid sick leave equal to the number of days the employee would normally work during a period of six weeks. During the first six months of employment, an employee is entitled to one day's paid sick leave for every 26 days worked.

The employer is not required to pay an employee if the employee has been absent from work for more than two consecutive days or on more than two occasions during an eight-week period and, on request by the employer, does not produce a medical certificate stating that the employee was unable to work for the duration of the employee's absence on account of sickness or injury.

11. **Maternity leave**

The employee is entitled to at least four consecutive months' maternity leave. The employer is not obliged to pay the domestic worker for the period for which she is off work due to her pregnancy. However the parties may agree that the domestic worker will receive part of or her entire salary/wage for the time that she is off due to pregnancy.

12. **Family responsibility leave**

Employees employed for longer than four months and for at least four days a week are entitled to take five days' paid family responsibility leave during each leave cycle when the employee's child is born, or when the employee's child is sick or in the event of the death of the employee's spouse or life partner or parent, adoptive parent, grandparent, child, adopted child, grandchild or sibling.

13. **Deduction from the remuneration**

The Sectoral Determination prohibits an employer from deducting any monies from the workers wages without his/her written permission. A deduction of not more than 10% of the wage may be deducted for a room or other accommodation provided it is kept in a good condition has at least one window and a door, which can be locked, and he/she has access to a bathroom.

14. **Other issues**

There are certain other issues which are not regulated by the Sectoral Determination such as probationary periods, right of entry to the employers premises, afternoons off, weekends off and pension schemes, medical aid schemes, training/school fees, funeral benefits and savings account, however the aforementioned may be negotiated between the parties and included in the contract of employment.

15. **Prohibition of Employment**

The Sectoral Determination prohibits employment of any person under the age of 15 and it is therefore important for an employer to verify the age of the domestic worker by requesting a copy of the identity document or birth certificate.

16. **Other conditions of employment**

There is no provision, which prevents any other conditions of employment being included in a contract of employment but any provision, which sets conditions, which are less favourable than those set by the Determination, would be invalid.

These guidelines are not meant to be a complete summary of the Sectoral Determination and/or legal advice. Should there be any doubt as to rights and/or obligations in terms of the Act or terms of any clause of the suggested Contract of Employment, such queries can be directed to the local office of the Department of Labour, who will gladly assist.

SAMPLE

AGRICULTURE/FARM WORKER CONTRACT OF EMPLOYMENT

MADE AND ENTERED INTO BY AND BETWEEN

______________________________	______________________________
(name of Employer)	(with address at)

Herein represented by ____ duly authorized hereto (hereinafter referred to as the *"Employer")*

AND

______________________________	______________________________
(name of Employee)	(with address at)
______________________________	______________________________
(identity number)	(mobile number)

(hereinafter referred to as the *"Employee")*

For further purposes of this agreement, the male shall import the female and vice versa, and reference to "company" shall include reference to "employer".

WHEREAS

1.1 The Employer appoints the employee to provide services and the employee accepts such appointment by the Employer.

1.2 The employee is able to provide the services required by the Employer and warrants that he is suitably organized, qualified and experienced in the provision of the services referred to and required in terms of this contract.

1.3 The parties hereto wish to record and reduce this agreement into writing, in order to constitute a written contract of employment.

WHEREBY THE PARTIES AGREE AS FOLLOWS:

1. INTRODUCTION

1.1 The Employer has offered employment to the employee, in a unique unpredictable and challenging employment environment.

1.2 Both parties agree unconditionally that this contract is of a commercial nature based on mutual reciprocity and the economic, business and financial interest of both parties.

1.3 The Employer appoints the employee to provide the services and the employee accepts such appointment.

1.4 The employee is able to provide services required by the Employer and warrants that he is suitably organized, qualified, and experienced in the provision of the services referred to and required in terms of this contract.

2. APPOINTMENT, DUTIES AND GUIDELINES

2.1 It is hereby confirmed that the employee has been offered and has accepted employment as a ___________ (job title) of ________ (premises/site/farm).

2.2 The Employer hereby appoints the employee to provide core services as follows:

2.2.1 ______
2.2.2 ______
2.2.3 ______
2.2.4 ______
2.2.5 ______
2.2.6 Other

2.3 The employee unconditionally confirms, recognizes and supports the complete flexibility of tasks, jobs and duties and will comply with all reasonable instructions, inclusive of the performance of additional duties and tasks as and when required by the Employer. The employee accepts that changes in work practices and working conditions will occur and be made by the giving of short notice. By accepting this offer of employment the employee agrees that he will be flexible in adapting to changes in working conditions, and that he will not be obstructive in response to changes to the terms and conditions hereof.

2.4 The employee implicitly agrees and promises that he:

2.4.1 is competent to perform the contractual obligations and the work employed for;

2.4.2 will perform all functions and activities assigned to the best of his ability and in an efficient manner;

2.4.3 will perform duties in accordance with Employer's policy, guidelines and instructions, custom and practice, as well as implied understandings;

2.4.4 guarantees that agreed performance and output targets required by the Employer will be met and achieved, and agrees that underperformance inclusive of inefficiency and incompetence, or the inability to achieve set standards, could lead to dismissal.

3. DURATION

3.1 This agreement will continue indefinitely, or until it terminates on the earliest of any of the following dates or events –

3.1.1 on ______ (date; or

3.1.2 upon completion of the project/work: ________________ (name of project work) with estimated completion time of ____________ (months/years);

3.1.3 upon completion of the purpose or tasks(s) for which the employee was appointed, as stipulated hereinabove.

4. WAGES AND CONDITIONS OF EMPLOYMENT

4.1 The employee shall be paid in cash/EFT on the last working day of every week/month	R________
4.2 The employee shall be entitled to the following allowances/ payment in kind:	
4.2.1 A weekly/monthly transport allowance of	R________
4.2.2 Meals per week/month to the value of	R________
4.2.3 Accommodation per week/month to the value of	R________
4.3 The total value of the above remuneration shall be	R________

4.4 Statutory conditions of employment are primarily set by the Sectoral Determination, essentially as follows:

4.4.1 Hours of work

The employee's weekly hours of work shall be -

(a) From Monday to Friday _________ (from) _________ (to); or

(b) In accordance with a weekly/fortnightly/monthly work/shift schedule

4.4.2 **Meal & Other Intervals**

The employee is entitled to a meal interval of 30 minutes, which does not form part of normal working hours. The Employer, entirely at his discretion, may make allowance for other intervals, which would be considered part of normal working hours.

4.4.3 **Overtime**

The employee agrees to work overtime, on Sundays or public holidays, when required, at prevailing overtime rates and at short notice.

4.4.4 **Sick Leave**

The employee is entitled to sick leave in accordance with applicable legislation. The employee will furthermore abide by any absenteeism rules implemented by the Employer to regulate sick leave and to prevent abuse of sick leave.

4.4.5 **Maternity and Paternity Leave**

The legislative provisions pertaining to maternity and paternity leave will apply.

4.4.6 **Public Holidays**

The employee will be entitled to all official public holidays on full pay. If an employee does not work on a public holiday, he shall receive normal payment for that day. If the employee works on a public holiday he shall be paid double.

4.4.7 **Annual Leave**

The employee is entitled to 21 (twenty-one) days paid leave after every 12 months of continuous service. Such leave is to be taken at times convenient to the Employer and the Employer may require the employee to take leave at such times as convenient to the Employer.

4.4.8 **Family Responsibility Leave**

The applicable statutory provisions will prevail.

4.4.9 **Deductions**

Deductions from salary shall be in accordance with statutory provisions.

5. HEALTH AND SAFETY

5.1 The obligation to ensure that the workplace is a safe and healthy environment conducive to maximal performance and productivity rests primarily on the Employer, with the employee fulfilling a supportive and ancillary function.

5.2 It is agreed that both the Employer and the employee have statutory safety and health duties and obligations, in addition to common law contractual duties of care and to adhere to safety and health protocol.

5.3 Statutory Regulations as well as the Employer's rules and guidelines in respect of the safety and health of employees and the population at large, must be taken into consideration in order to achieve and to further enhance a safe and healthy work environment. Breach of the aforementioned could result in discipline and dismissal.

6. **COMPANY RULES AND REGULATIONS**

6.1 Schedule 8 to the Labour Relationship Act: "A Code of Good Conduct - Dismissal", is applicable as a Guideline Code to this agreement in respect of -

6.1.1 Disciplinary measures
6.1.2 Dismissal
6.1.3 Probation (if applicable)
6.1.4 Poor Work Performance
6.1.5 Incapacity and ill-health
6.1.6 Medical incapacity

6.2 The Employer shall be entitled to require the employee to submit to:

6.2.1 Medical examination and/or medical testing
6.2.2 Alcohol testing
6.2.3 Drug and or any illegal substance testing
6.2.4 Polygraph testing
6.2.5 Security clearances

The employee consents to any of the above tests and/or processes to be conducted and agrees that he will not refuse instructions in this regard and that he will not be obstructive in any manner whatsoever.

6.3 The employee agrees to submit to searches of person and possessions by persons designated by the Employer as where and when necessary, and at the discretion of management.

6.4 During the first 6 (six) months of employment, the employee is entitled to 1 (one) day's paid sick leave for every 26 (twenty-six) days worked. After a period of 6 (six) months, the employee will be entitled to 30 (thirty) days sick leave over a sick leave cycle of 36 (thirty-six) months.

6.5 Should the employee be unable to attend work because of illness, the employee is required to notify his manager before 10h00 on that day.

6.6 The Employer is not required to pay the employee sick leave in the event of:

6.6.1 The employee being absent from work for more than 2 (two) consecutive days; and/or

6.6.2 The employee being absent from work more than 2 (two) occasions during an 8 (eight) week period; and/or

6.6.3 On request by the Employer, failure by the employee to produce a medical certificate stating that he was unable to work for the duration of his absence on account of sickness or injury; and or

6.6.4 The employee abusing sick leave provisions

7. TERMINATION OF EMPLOYMENT/BREACH OF CONTRACT

7.1 During the first four weeks of employment either party can terminate this agreement with one week written notice. After four weeks of employment either party can terminate this agreement with four weeks written notice.

7.2 The employee will be liable for summary dismissal in the following instances:

7.2.1 Damage to equipment, sabotage, causing of fires, poor work performance, defiance, rejection of control of authority, theft, dishonesty, poaching, assault, provocation, intimidation, subversive activities inclusive of criminal conduct, absence without leave, poorly explained absenteeism, abscondment, desertion, incompetence, gross negligence, insubordination and disrespect, intoxication, disregard of safety rules, damage to goods and or property, unprocedural strike action or go-slows, deceitful conduct, and any conduct that results in the breakdown of the employment relationship.

8. RETIREMENT AGE

8.1 The parties specifically agree that the normal retirement age is at _____ years of age. The employee's service shall for this reason automatically terminate at the end of the year in which he reaches the agreed retirement age.

8.2 In terms of Employer policy having reached the mandatory retirement age of ___ will constitute a termination by operation of law and same will not constitute a dismissal. The Employer has discretion to allow any employee to work beyond the age of ____ and each retiree will be treated on individual merit and circumstances.

9. FORCE MAJEURE

Neither party will be liable for the delay or failure to perform any obligation and or undertaking in terms of this contract in the event and to the extent that such delay or failure is caused by force majeure including but not limited to an act of God, fire, lightening, earthquake, drought, flood, crop failure, general emergency, insurrection, civil disorder, war, military operations, pandemic, act of terrorism or the declaration of a state of emergency or a national disaster.

10. AGREEMENT

10.1 The employee warrants that he is not suffering from any medical defect, disability and or ailment which will impair him from carrying out of his obligations in terms of this contract. Should the employee be in breach of this warranty the Employer shall have the option to terminate employment forthwith.

10.2 The failure of the employee to produce employment documentation such as security clearances, an identity document and/or passport, work permit documentation, educational certificates and/or proof of trade qualifications, upon request of the Company, could also result in the termination of this contract. In addition, this contract could be considered void *ab initio,* as a result.

Thus done and signed at ____________________ on this _____ day of ____________ 20__.

As a witness:	For and on behalf of **the Employer** by
______________________________	______________________________
	Who warrants authority hereto

Thus done and signed at ____________________ on this _____ day of ____________ 20__.

As a witness:	The **employee**
______________________________	______________________________

SAMPLE

SEASONAL EMPLOYMENT CONTRACT OF EMPLOYMENT

MADE AND ENTERED INTO BY AND BETWEEN

____________________	____________________
(name of Employer)	(with address at)

Herein represented by ____________________ duly authorized hereto (hereinafter referred to as the *"Employer")*

AND

____________________	____________________
(name of Employee)	(with address at)
____________________	____________________
(identity number)	(mobile number)

(hereinafter referred to as the *"Employee")*

For further purposes of this agreement, the male shall import the female and vice versa, and reference to "company" shall include reference to "employer".

WHEREAS

1.1 The Company appoints the employee to provide services and the employee accepts such appointment by the Company.

1.2 The employee is able to provide the services required by the Company and warrants that he is suitably organized, qualified and experienced in the provision of the services referred to and required in terms of this contract.

1.3 The parties hereto wish to record and reduce this agreement into writing, in order to constitute a written contract of employment.

WHEREBY THE PARTIES AGREE AS FOLLOWS:

1. INTRODUCTION

1.1 The Employer is in need of the specified services of the employee, in a unique as well as challenging employment environment subject to seasonal changes, vagaries of the weather and unpredictable employment conditions.

1.2 Both parties agree unconditionally that this contract is of a commercial nature based on mutual reciprocity and the economic, business and financial interest of both parties.

1.3 This contract is for seasonal work primarily in the agricultural, fishing and food industries.

2. APPOINTMENT, DUTIES AND GUIDELINES

2.1 It is hereby confirmed that the employee has been offered and has accepted seasonal employment as a ___________ (job title) of ________ (contract/premises/farm).

2.2 The Employer hereby appoints the employee to provide core services as follows:

2.2.1 ______
2.2.2 ______
2.2.3 ______
2.2.4 ______
2.2.5 ______
2.2.6 Other

2.3 The employee unconditionally confirms, recognizes and supports the complete flexibility of tasks, jobs and duties and will comply with all reasonable instructions, inclusive of the performance of additional duties and tasks as and when required by the Employer. The employee accepts that changes in work practices and working conditions will occur and be made by the giving of short notice. By accepting this offer of employment the employee agrees that he will be flexible in adapting to changes in working conditions, and that he will not be obstructive in response to changes to the terms and conditions hereof.

2.4 The employee implicitly agrees and promises that he/she:

2.4.1 is competent to perform the contractual obligations and the work employed for;

2.4.2 will perform all functions and activities assigned to the best of his/her ability and in an efficient manner;

2.4.3 will perform duties in accordance with the Employer's policies, guidelines and instructions, custom and practice, as well as implied understandings;

2.4.4 guarantees that agreed performance and output targets required by the Employer will be met and achieved, and agrees that underperformance, inclusive of inefficiency and incompetence, or the inability to achieve set standards, could lead to dismissal.

3. DURATION

3.1 The employee accepts temporary employment for the _____ season, which extends from _____ (date) to approximately _____ (dates), as and when work is available.

3.2 Whereas the Employer's business requires various factors to be in place for a continuous work activity, (for example favourable weather conditions, the degree of ripeness of products, the availability of production resources, market conditions etc.) there may be times when no work is available or possible for the employee.

3.3 The Employer shall therefore only pay the employee if his/her services are required and utilized.

4. WAGES AND CONDITIONS OF EMPLOYMENT - SEASONAL EMPLOYMENT

4.1 Any applicable Sectoral Determination in respect of minimum conditions shall apply to this contract of employment.

4.2 The following basic wage and conditions of employment also apply:

4.2.1 **Wage**: A basic wage of R______ per hour worked (or piece work at current rates) payment weekly/two-weekly in cash/per electronic transfer

4.2.2 **Working hours**: An average of 45 hours per week in a five-day working week

4.2.3 **Overtime pay**: Monday to Friday = 1 ½ x the basic hourly wage for hours worked in excess of the normal daily hours

4.2.4 **Sunday work**: As determined in the applicable Sectoral Determination

4.2.5 **Inclement weather stoppage**: The Employer shall, by giving the employee at least one hour's notice, decide whether work cannot be performed due to unfavourable weather or other unforeseen circumstances

4.2.6 **Leave**: One day's leave for every 17 days worked shall be paid out on termination of the contract where the duration of the contract exceeds four months

4.2.7 **Sick leave:** Paid sick leave of one working day for every 26 days in respect of which the employee was entitled to payment, provided that an appropriate medical certificate is submitted for absence of more than 2 (two) days, or on more than 2 (two) occasions within eight weeks.

4.2.8 **Public holidays:** If any public holiday falls on a normal working day within a period of unbroken service, the employee shall be entitled to a day off on full pay, and if the holiday falls on a Sunday, the employee shall have the subsequent Monday off on full pay. If the employee works on such a public holiday, he/she shall be paid at least double his/her daily wage, unless the majority of employees, at the Employer's request, agree to exchange that day with another normal working day within a reasonable period of time

4.3 The employee authorizes the Employer to deduct any statutory amount, or any amount owed to the Employer, from the Employee's wage or from any other monies due to the employee.

5. HEALTH AND SAFETY

5.1 The obligation to ensure that the workplace is a safe and healthy environment conducive to maximal performance and productivity rests primarily on the Employer. The employee agrees to comply with all directives and/or instructions implemented by the Employer for safety and health purposes.

5.2 Both parties acknowledge that the Employer and the employee have statutory safety and health duties and obligations, in addition to common law, contractual duties of care and to adhere to safety and health protocol.

5.3 The employee agrees that Statutory Regulations as well as the Employer's rules and guidelines in respect of the safety and health of employees and the population at large, must be taken into consideration in order to achieve and to further enhance a safe and healthy work environment. Disregard for safety and health rules and regulations could result in discipline and dismissal.

6. EMPLOYER RULES AND REGULATIONS

6.1 Schedule 8 to the Labour Relations Act: "A Code of Good Conduct - Dismissal" is applicable as a Guideline core to this agreement in respect of:

6.1.1 Disciplinary measures
6.1.2 Dismissal
6.1.3 Poor Work Performance
6.1.4 Incapacity and Ill-Health
6.1.5 Medical Incapacity

6.2 The Employer shall be entitled to require the employee to submit to:

6.2.1 Medical examination and/or medical testing
6.2.2 Alcohol testing
6.2.3 Drug and or any illegal substance testing

6.2.4 Polygraph testing
6.2.5 Security clearances

The employee consents to any of the above tests and/or processes to be conducted and agrees that he will not refuse instructions in this regard and that he will not be obstructive in any manner whatsoever.

6.3 The employee agrees to submit to searches of person and possessions by persons designated by the Employer as where and when necessary, and at the discretion of management.

6.4 Should the employee be unable to attend work because of illness, the employee is required to notify his/her manager before 10h00 on that day.

6.5 The Employer is not required to pay the employee sick leave in the event of:

6.5.1 The employee being absent from work for more than 2 (two) consecutive days; and/or,
6.5.2 The employee being absent from work more than 2 (two) occasions during an 8 (eight) week period; and/or
6.5.3 On request by the Employer, failure by the employee to produce a medical certificate stating that he or she was unable to work for the duration of his/her absence on account of sickness or injury; and or
6.5.4 The employee abusing sick leave provisions

7. TERMINATION OF EMPLOYMENT/BREACH OF CONTRACT

7.1 During the first four weeks of employment either party can terminate this agreement with one week written notice. After four weeks of employment either party can terminate this agreement with four weeks written notice.

In the case where an employee is illiterate notice may be given by that employee verbally.

7.2 The employee will be liable for summary dismissal in the following instances:

7.2.1 Damage to equipment, sabotage, causing of fires, poor work performance, defiance, rejection of control of authority, theft, dishonesty, poaching, assault, provocation, intimidation, subversive activities inclusive of criminal conduct, absence without leave, poorly explained absenteeism, abscondment, desertion, incompetence, gross negligence, insubordination and disrespect, intoxication, disregard of safety rules, damage to goods and or property, unprocedural strike action or go-slows, deceitful conduct, and any conduct that results in the breakdown of the employment relationship.

8. FORCE MAJEURE

Neither party will be liable for the delay or failure to perform any obligation and or undertaking in terms of this contract in the event and to the extent that such delay or failure is caused by force majeure including but not limited to an act of God, fire, lightening, earthquake, drought, flood, crop failure, general emergency, insurrection, civil disorder, war, military operations, pandemic, act of terrorism or the declaration of a state of emergency or a national disaster.

9. AGREEMENT

9.1 The employee warrants that he is not suffering from any medical defect, disability and or ailment which will impair him from carrying out his obligations in terms of this contract. Should the employee be in breach of this warranty the Employer shall have the option to terminate employment forthwith.

9.2 The failure of the employee to produce employment documentation such as security clearances, an identity document and/or passport, work permit documentation, educational certificates and/or proof of trade qualifications, upon request of the Employer, could also result in the termination of this contract. In addition, this contract could be considered void *ab inito* as a result.

Thus done and signed at ________________ on this ____ day of __________ 20__.

As a witness:	For and on behalf of **the Employer** by
______________________	______________________
	Who warrants authority hereto

Thus done and signed at ________________ on this ____ day of __________ 20__.

As a witness:	The **employee**
______________________	______________________

SAMPLE

INDEPENDENT CONTRACTOR'S AGREEMENT

between

____

(the "Company")

and

____

(the "Contractor")

IT IS AGREED AS FOLLOWS:

1. INTRODUCTION

1.1 The Company may have a need from time to time to sub-contract services.

1.2 The Company appoints the Independent Contractor on the terms and conditions recorded in this agreement in order to assist the Company in the following areas:-

DESCRIPTION OF SERVICES TO BE RENDERED BY THE CONTRACTOR (EXAMPLE)

1.2.1 General messenger duties inclusive of delivery duties as an when required.

1.2.2 Searching and purchase of components and consumables at short notice.

1.2.3 Other: ____

1.3 It is recorded and agreed that the Contractor will not render personal services to the Company and that the Company has no control and authority over the Contractor's business.

2. APPOINTMENT AS AN INDEPENDENT CONTRACTOR

2.1 The Company accordingly hereby appoints the Contractor who accepts the appointment to assist as and when necessary, and as required.

2.2 It is recorded that nothing in this agreement, whether express or implied, shall be construed as creating the relationship of employer and employee between the parties, and that the Contractor is not solely reliant on the Company for an income.

2.3 The contractor will only be utilized as and when it is necessary to do so, at the sole and entire discretion of the Company, and is at liberty to provide services to any other client of such Contractor.

3. **PERIOD**

Subject to clause 11 this agreement shall remain in force for an indefinite period. This agreement shall prevail at all times for so long as the Contractor renders services to the Company.

4. **PAYMENT FOR SERVICES**

4.1 The Company will pay to the Contractor on the production of a VAT tax invoice, within 7 days of the presentation of the invoice.

4.2 No other fees and/or expenses will be paid to the Contractor unless such fees and/or expenses have been approved in advance by the Company in writing. The Contractor shall be solely responsible for any and all taxes, Social Security contributions or payments, disability insurance, unemployment taxes, and other payroll type taxes applicable to the services so provided by the Contractor.

5. **PAYMENT OF FEES CONDITIONAL**

5.1 In the event of the Contractor not complying with the terms of this agreement in any respect whatsoever inclusive of not rendering agreed services the fee due to the Contractor shall not be due or payable to the Contractor

5.2 The Company shall be entitled to either deduct or set-off from the Contractor's fee any amount that may be owed to the Company by the Contractor for any reason whatsoever.

6. **AUTHORITY**

6.2.1 The authority of the Contractor in terms of this agreement shall be limited to the services to be provided on behalf of the Company in the execution of its business.

6.2.2 The Contractor shall not have the authority to incur any debt or other liability or to obtain any credit facilities either in the name of on behalf of the Company without having obtained the prior written authority of the Company ("written authority" for the purposes of this clause shall include a telefax authority signed by a duly authorised representative of the Company).

6.2.3 The Contractor shall frankly, timeously and if necessary, advise suppliers and other relevant persons that the Contractor does business with, but he has no authority to bind the Company.

7. **IMPLIED WARRANTY OF EXPERTISE/OBLIGATIONS**

7.1 The Contractor guarantees that he can fulfil in the services so contracted to him and that he shall observe the following standards in the conduct of his business for the Company i.e. to:-

7.1.1 carry out the independent services rendered in a courteous, competent, efficient and cost effective manner, as per paragraph 1.2 herein above;

7.1.2 attend all meetings at which the Contractor's attendance is required by the Company, on reasonable notification.

8. **CONFIDENTIALITY**

8.1 The Contractor may have access to proprietary, private and/or otherwise confidential information ("Confidential Information") of the Company. Confidential Information shall mean all non-public information which constitutes, relates or refers to the operation of the business of the Company, including without limitation, all financial, investment, operational, personnel, sales, marketing, managerial and statistical information of the Company, and any and all trade secrets, customer lists, or pricing information of the Company.

8.2 The Contractor shall not disclose any confidential information whatsoever and the Company reserves the right to institute legal proceedings against the Contractor in such event. The Contractor agrees to such proceedings should it become necessary to protect the interests of the Company.

9. **INDEMNITY**

The Contractor hereby indemnifies and holds the Company harmless against all claims, demands, fines, penalties, actions, proceedings, judgments, damages, losses, costs, expenses, or other liabilities caused, whether negligently or otherwise, to the Company by the non-observance or non-compliance by the Contractor of the duties and obligations under this agreement.

10. NO EMPLOYMENT RELATIONSHIP

10.1 The Contractor acknowledges and agrees that:-

10.1.1 the relationship between the parties is not one of employer and employee; but that of independent contractor;

10.1.2 Employment Legislation accordingly does not apply to this agreement, and the Contractor will acquire no rights whatsoever in respect of such Legislation;

10.1.3 the nature of this agreement has been explained to the Contractor prior to the Contractor's signature to and acceptance of this agreement;

11. TERMINATION

11.1 Either party may terminate this agreement by giving 14 (fourteen) days notice of such termination to the other party.

11.2 The Company will be entitled to terminate this agreement forthwith for material breach and should the Contractor:-

11.2.1 fail to meet/comply with the Company's service standards; and/or fail to meet performance standards as well as requisite standards of output;

11.2.2 acts unlawfully and/or commits a criminal offence;

11.2.3 competes with the Company;

11.2.4 falsify any documents or records;

11.2.5 acts in a dishonest, fraudulent or deceitful manner;

11.2.6 commits any act which, in the reasonable opinion of the Company adversely affects or is likely to affect the business and/or the reputation of the Company.

12. DISPUTES

In the event of any dispute that may arise as a result of the provisions of this agreement the dispute shall be referred to Arbitration in terms of the provisions of the Arbitration Act.

13. ADDRESSES

13.1 For the purposes of this agreement, including the giving of notices and the serving of legal process, the parties select domicilium citandi et executandi at the addresses recorded below:-

____

(the "Company")

____

____

____

____

____

(The "Contractor")

____

____

____

____

14. **GENERAL**

14.1 Each party shall give the other party 30 (thirty) days' written notice of a change of address. The other party shall acknowledge in writing receipt of such notice.

14.2 No indulgence granted by a party shall constitute a waiver of any of that party's rights under this agreement. Accordingly, that party shall not be precluded, as a consequence of having granted such indulgence, from exercising any rights against the other which may have or may arise.

14.3 No agreement varying, adding to, deleting from or cancelling this agreement, shall be effective unless reduced to writing and signed by or on behalf of the parties.

14.4 This agreement and the documents referred to herein contain the entire agreement between the parties and neither party shall be bound by any undertaking, representations or warranties not recorded herein.

14.5 This agreement shall be interpreted and implemented in accordance with the laws of the Republic of South Africa.

14.6 For the purposes of this agreement any reference to the male gender shall include a reference to the female gender where applicable.

SIGNED at ____________________ on this the _______ day of ______________ 20___.

____

For and on behalf of the Company he being duly authorised hereto

AS A WITNESS

____

SIGNED at ____________________ on this the ______ day of ______________ 202__.

SAMPLE

NOTES ON RESTRAINT OF TRADE AND CONFIDENTIALITY

1. The prohibition on the employee not to engage in competitive, alternative employment and business activity, during as well as post-employment, is at best a legal minefield, the assessment of which depends on the individual circumstances of each case, the contents of a restraint of trade and/or agreement, and the prevailing economic circumstances of the time.

2. For a restraint of trade (and the prohibition to conduct business in certain specific circumstances) to be enforceable as well as legitimate, there has to be a protectable interest for instance, confidential information or trade customers. The Courts would then take into account the interests of both parties and whether there was an issue of public interest or constitutional values that affected the agreement, for instance the need for the employee to work.

3. Bad faith and/or nefarious post employment conduct inclusive of competing with the employer and the poaching and/or soliciting of staff can also be prohibited by means of contractual obligations.

4. For a restraint agreement to be held to be enforceable an employer would have to:

   4.1 have an interest deserving of protection;
   4.2 demonstrate the real possibility of the protected interest being threatened post termination of employment;
   4.3 demonstrate that the protected interest is worthy of protection; and
   4.4 demonstrate that there is no public policy aspect that would cause the restraint agreement to be held to be unenforceable;
   4.5 rely on a clearly worded restraint of trade agreement that compromises the employee legally.

5. The restraint of trade agreement should be as specific as possible. It should not be too wide in duration, product range or in geographical area in the specific circumstances.

6. All of the above mentioned factors will be determined by the courts as a whole taking into account the particular facts. This will be done by means of an enquiry in terms of:

   6.1 The nature of the activity to be prevented;
   6.2 The area of operation of the restraint;
   6.3 The duration thereof;

6.4 The interests of both parties and their "relative positions of strength";

6.5 The general economic circumstances at the time of the restraint being enforced, and whether the employer had acted reasonably.

6.6 There are many different styles of restraint agreements and clauses, some lengthy and quite complicated whilst others are short and concise.

The following is a basic, sample Restraint of Trade Agreement or clause:

RESTRAINT OF TRADE

1. The employee is prohibited to supply any goods, information, or to render any services to any clients, their employees or representatives, suppliers or any employee of the Company except as may be required in the course of his employment.

2. In the course of the employee's duties, he will be exposed to and or privy to information of a personal, private or confidential nature relating to the Company and or its products. All such information is proprietary in nature and is the exclusive property of the Company.

3. The employee is expressly and specifically forbidden to disclose such information to or discuss it with any person in the Company's employ or outside other than with his superior, and immediate co-employees who are authorized to deal with these matters. The employee is further specifically prohibited from making use of any such information after his contract with the Company has been terminated.

4. Inventions and or other innovations may fall within the scope of an employee's employment. Such inventions or other innovations are deemed to be the property of the Company and the employee will assign such inventions and innovations to the Company upon request. The employee will also sign any forms necessary in the protection of such inventions and other innovations in Southern Africa and elsewhere.

5. Corporate information is generated, obtained and contained by various methods, e.g., verbal communication, documentation, internet, email, telephone, social media, cell phone and computers. This corporate information is for the sole benefit of the Company.

6. The employee fully recognizes and acknowledges that the Company has intellectual property assets and has established measures and assigned responsibilities to protect those assess from abuse, loss, theft, unauthorized modification and disclosure.

7. In order to protect the Company's corporate information and intellectual property and assets, the Company reserves the right (and the employee authorizes the Company) j to monitor and or intercept email transmissions, internet usage, computer utilization, telephone conversations, and social media, as may be required to protect the Company's interests.

8. To avoid any conflict of interest, the employee agrees not to engage directly and or indirectly in any alternative employment whilst remaining in the Company's employ, without written permission of the Company. The specific intent of this contract is that the employee remains loyal to and acts in the best interests of the Company and devotes all of his time, skills and knowledge in the interests of the Company at all times.

9. The employee acknowledges that the Company has an extremely high degree of competition and that it is imperative that all such information, not published by the Company to the general public constitutes trade secrets, confidential and proprietary to the Company.

10. Accordingly, the employee as well as every employee is required specifically not to disclose, during and following his employment, the production, marketing, professional and organizational secrets or other trade and/or confidential information of the Company, its affiliated companies, or its customers to a competitor or third party.

11. This obligation shall remain in effect for as long as the trade and/or confidential information remains a secret and privileged, or in any event, for a period of at least 12 (twelve) months from the date of termination of the employee's service with the Company. The employee unconditionally agrees that he will not provide services of whatsoever kind, to any competitors of the Company, and which could be detrimental to the interests of the Company, for the period referred to hereinabove and within the geographical area(s) of:

    (a) ______________________: and/or

    (b) ______________________; and/or

    (c) ______________________; and/or

    (d) ______________________.

12. Breach of confidentiality could result in summary dismissal and or legal action of whatsoever nature against the employee and or his associates, with a resultant Court Order to interdict and or to restrain him and/or them. The employee is in agreement that the Company is entitled by law to pursue any claims against him and or his associates at the time of the event of the alleged breaches of confidentiality and or restraint of trade.

13. The employee is not entitled to receive any gifts, money and or benefits from clients or prospective clients without the prior approval of the Company.

14. The employee unconditionally agrees not to poach and/or to solicit any of the staff of the Company during his employment, as well as for a period of 12 (twelve) months after the termination of his employment.

KEY PERFORMANCE AREAS ("KPA's") AND PERFORMANCE AGREEMENT

- **POSITION DESCRIPTION DOCUMENT/JOB CONTENT AND COMPLIANCE STANDARDS**

Acknowledgement of Induction/Key Performance Areas Form

Acknowledgement of Induction/Key Performance Areas

I, ____________________ (full names of employee), employed as ____________________ (job title), acknowledge and recognize that I have been fully informed by my employer in respect of my KPA's, conditions as well as contract of employment, and that I have been inducted in the following matters:

1.	Job Contents/Standards of Performance/KPA's	**YES/NO**
2.	Contract of Employment and Competency Guarantee	**YES/NO**
3.	Management Structures/Control and Authority	**YES/NO**
4.	Conditions of Employment	**YES/NO**
5.	Disciplinary Code and Procedure/Schedule 8 LRA Code of Good Practice: Dismissal	**YES/NO**
6.	General Office and/or Premises Housekeeping Rules and Regulations	**YES/NO**
7.	Standards of Performance	**YES/NO**
8.	Conduct and Attitude	**YES/NO**
9.	Safety and Health	**YES/NO**
10.	Communications inclusive of Electronic Communication and Internet Rules	**YES/NO**
11.	Conduct Off-Company Premises/After Hours Conduct	**YES/NO**
12.	Absenteeism inclusive of Reporting and taking of Sick Leave Rules	**YES/NO**
13.	Resolution of Grievances and/or Misunderstandings	**YES/NO**
14.	Maintenance of the Employment Trust Relationship and Obligations to be Honest and Transparent at all times	**YES/NO**

I further acknowledge and agree that I fully understand and accept the facts that were communicated to me properly and that I am fully aware of all the conditions explained to me.

I agree that this acknowledgement inclusive of the attached schedule of KPAs, will be binding in law and that the employer has complied with its obligations in respect of Item 9 of the Code of Good Practice: Dismissal – Labour Relations Act.

Signed on the ________ day of ______________ 20____ at ________________________.

____________________________________	____________________________________
(employee)	(management)
____________________________________	____________________________________
(witness)	(witness)

SCHEDULE OF KPA's AND STANDARDS OF OUTPUT

Job Title: ____________________

A. KEY PERFORMANCE AREAS ("KPA's")

The following are the main KPA's of the abovementioned position, and expected standards of performance have been discussed with the employee.

LIST OF KPA's	EXPECTED STANDARDS OF PERFORMANCE
1.	
2.	
3.	
4.	
5.	

B. COMPETENCY AND PERFORMANCE GUARANTEES

The following undertakings are applicable:

COMPETENCY GUARANTEE

You implicitly agree and promise that you are competent to perform your contractual obligations and that you will perform your duties in an efficient manner in accordance with company policy, guidelines and instructions, customer and practice, as well as implied understandings.

IMPLIED WARRANTY OF SUITABILITY

- You unconditionally guarantee that you are suitable to perform the work for which you were employed and guarantee that you perform all functions and activities assigned to you to the best of your abilities.
- In addition, you guarantee that you will meet the standards of performance and output required by the company.
- You agree that under-performance or inability to achieve set standards could lead to dismissal.
- The company's policy in respect of poor work performance is one of zero tolerance and employees who do not meet requisite standards may be dismissed.

NATURE OF THE EMPLOYMENT CONTRACT

- Both parties (i.e. you and the company) agree unconditionally that this contract is of a commercial nature based on mutual reciprocity and the economic interests of both parties.
- Should it become apparent either to yourself or the Company that there is not mutual benefit that results from this contract of the employment relationship, then either party will be entitled to terminate the contract summarily.

EMPLOYMENT DUTIES AND OBLIGATIONS

The company adheres to fundamental norms of order through professional management and the responsible conduct and attitude of all concerned. You will be required therefore, to attend to your duties diligently, in the best interests of the company and in a manner that will not discredit or compromise the company whatsoever. The company's written and implied rules and standards in respect of conduct and behaviour, as well as capacity and performance shall accordingly apply. The company provides for a fair and equitable system of employment relations which will provide you with security of employment as well as the opportunity to discuss work-related matters as and when necessary.

You undertake to:

1. Carry out all such functions and duties as are from time to time assigned to you and as are reasonable and lawful;
2. Obey and comply with all lawful and reasonable instructions given to you by your superior;
3. Be true and faithful to the company in all dealings and transactions relating to the business and interests of the company and to use your best endeavours to protect and promote the business, reputation and good name of the company;
4. Submit to the management or to any person nominated by management such information and reports as may be required of you in connection with the performance of your duties and the business of the company.
5. Devote the whole of your time and attention during the company working hours and such additional time as the exigencies of company business may require, to the business affairs of the company and to your duties in terms of your employment with the company; and
6. Meet performance and output targets.

I agree that this acknowledgement will be binding in law and that I am fit and able to do the job.

Signedonthe________dayof________________20____at_________________________.

_________________________________ _________________________________

(employee) (management)

_________________________________ _________________________________

(witness) (witness)

CONVENTIONAL PENALTIES ACT NO. 15 OF 1962

[ASSENTED TO 5 MARCH, 1962]
[DATE OF COMMENCEMENT: 16 MARCH, 1962]
(English text signed by the State President)

as amended by

General Law Amendment Act, No. 102 of 1967
[with effect from 21 June, 1967]
Justice Laws Rationalisation Act, No. 18 of 1996
[with effect from 1 April 1997]
General Law Amendment Act, No. 49 of 1996
[with effect from 4 October 1996]
National Credit Act, No. 34 of 2005
[with effect from 1 June, 2006, unless otherwise indicated]

GENERAL NOTICE

Conflicting legislation: S. 172 (1) of the National Credit Act, No. 34 of 2005 determines that the provisions of the National Credit Act, No. 34 of 2005, in so far as it applies to a credit agreement, prevail to the extent of the conflict.

ACT

To provide for the enforceability of penalty stipulations, including stipulations based on pre-estimates of damage, and of forfeiture clauses.

ARRANGEMENT OF SECTIONS

1. **Stipulations for penalties in case of breach of contract to be enforceable.-**
(1) A stipulation, hereinafter referred to as a penalty stipulation, whereby it is provided that any person shall, in respect of an act or omission in conflict with a contractual obligation, be liable to pay a sum of money or to deliver or perform anything for the benefit of any other person, hereinafter referred to as a creditor, either by way of a penalty or as liquidated damages, shall, subject to the provisions of this Act, be capable of being enforced in any competent court.

(2) Any sum of money for the payment of which or anything for the delivery or performance of which a person may so become liable, is in this Act referred to as a penalty.

2. **Prohibition on cumulation of remedies and limitation on recovery of penalties in respect of defects or delay.-**
(1) A creditor shall not be entitled to recover in respect of an act or omission which is the subject of a penalty stipulation, both the penalty and damages, or, except where the relevant contract expressly so provides, to recover damages in lieu of the penalty.

(2) A person who accepts or is obliged to accept defective or non-timeous performance shall not be entitled to recover a penalty in respect of the defect or delay, unless the penalty was expressly stipulated for in respect of that defect or delay.

3. **Reduction of excessive penalty.-**
If upon the hearing of a claim for a penalty, it appears to the court that such penalty is out of proportion to the prejudice suffered by the creditor by reason of the act or omission in respect of which the penalty was stipulated, the court may reduce the penalty to such extent as it may consider equitable in the circumstances: Provided that in determining the extent of such prejudice the court shall take into consideration not only the creditor's proprietary interest, but every other rightful interest which may be affected by the act or omission in question.

4. **Provisions as to penalty stipulations also apply in respect of forfeiture stipulations.-**
A stipulation whereby it is provided that upon withdrawal from an agreement by a party thereto under circumstances specified therein, any other party thereto shall forfeit the right to claim restitution of anything performed by him in terms of the agreement, or shall, notwithstanding the withdrawal, remain liable for the performance of anything thereunder, shall have effect to the extent and subject to the conditions prescribed in sections one to three, inclusive, as if it were a penalty stipulation.

5. ......

[S. 5 substituted by s. 18 (1) of Act No. 102 of 1967 and by s. 4 of Act No. 18 of 1996 and repealed by s. 172 (2) of Act No. 34 of 2005.]

6. ......

[S. 6 repealed by s. 1 of Act No. 49 of 1996.]

7. **Short title.-**
This Act shall be called the Conventional Penalties Act, 1962.

SAMPLE PENALTY CLAUSE

EMPLOYER RIGHTS: TERMINATION OF EMPLOYMENT AND REPAYMENT OF COSTS AND EXPENDITURE, TRAINING AND DEVELOPMENT

1. This clause shall only apply in the instance of terminations of employment during the initial training period of the employee and one year thereafter, which period will be a period of 36 months, and the provisions of the CPA shall apply.
2. The employer shall, in order to advance and promote the training and experience of the employee, provide for the employee to attend extensive in-house training.
3. The attendance at this training by the employee shall be considered to be in-occupation training of the employee.
4. It is recorded and agreed that the total value of the in-occupation training contemplated by this agreement, which includes time, expertise and actual disbursements expended by the employer, shall be a sum of R XXX. The table below reflects the training costs over the three (3) years.

   4.1 *Year 1 [Mentoring and Training R XXX]*
   4.2 *Year 2 [Mentoring and Training R XXX]*
   4.3 *Year 3 [Mentoring and Training R XXX]*

   Total costs of Training R XXX

5. In exchange for the in-occupation training provided by the employer to the employee in terms of this agreements, the employee agrees and undertakes as follows:

   5.1 the employee shall serve the employer for a minimum period of at least 3 (three) years;
   5.2 in the event of the employment of the employee with the employer terminating for any cause or reason whatsoever, be it resignation, dismissal or any other form of termination of employment, prior to the expiry of the time period in terms of clause 5.1 above, then and in such

event the employee shall immediately be obliged and required to pay the sum of (i) R XXX in the event of the employee serves the employer for a period of less than 1 (one) year completed service; (ii) R XXX in the event of the employee serves the employer for a period of less than 2 (two) years completed service; and (iii) R XXX in the event of the employee serves the employer for a period of less than 3 (three) years completed service, to the employer;

5.3 the sums set out in the above paragraph shall be immediately due, owing and payable by the employee to the employer with effect from the date of termination of the employment of the employee with the employer;

5.4 upon expiry of this 3 (three) year time limit in terms of this agreement, the employee's liability to pay the said sums to the employer shall terminate and be expunged;

5.5 insofar as the payment by the employee to the employer in terms of this agreement may be considered or deemed to be a penalty clause as contemplated by the CPA, the employee hereby and herewith acknowledges and agrees that such penalty clause is fair and reasonable, and that should the employee at any stage wish to allege the contrary, the employee shall have the onus to prove that such penalty clause is not fair and reasonable;

5.6 this agreement also serves as written consent by the employee in terms of the Basic Conditions of Employment Act to deduct the amount, or any part therefore, payment by the employee to the employer in terms of this agreement, from any final payment, salary or benefit due by the employer to the employee upon termination of employment by the employee with the employer.

SAMPLE

WORKING FROM HOME ("WFH") POLICY AND PROCEDURE

1. POLICY BRIEF AND PURPOSE

1.1 This WFH policy and procedure outlines guidelines for employees and management who work from a location other than the employer's offices. Employees may work remotely on a permanent or temporary basis.

1.2 Terms and conditions as per existing contracts of employment will continue to apply in the normal course of business and the employment relationship.

1.3 In order to achieve and to maintain efficiency all employees are subject to the complete flexibility of tasks, jobs and duties and are required to comply with all instructions, inclusive of the performance of additional duties as and when required by the Company. WFH employees need to be flexible and adaptable to change in order to ensure operational excellence, competitiveness and efficiency.

1.4 Major variations in contractual obligations will be changed by agreement and/or by the issuing of standard operating procedures ("SOP's").

2. SCOPE

2.1 This policy applies to employees whose primary work location is not at the offices, and only work remotely from home.

2.2 WFH employees must be treated equally and without discrimination, and terms and conditions of employment must be fair, and at least equivalent to those who are not working from home. WFH employees will be afforded the same opportunities for promotion, development and training and be equally eligible for other forms of flexible working.

2.3 WFH will have no adverse differential effects by gender, age, disability or race.

3. SAFETY AND HEALTH

3.1 A person conducting a business or undertaking is accountable for the health and safety of the home workplace in the same way as they are for a conventional workplace.

3.2 There are specific risks associated with working from home that must be taken into consideration. In this regard the employer will make every reasonable effort to ensure that WFH employees:

3.2.1 Are included in all health and safety consultation;

3.2.2 Have a suitable workspace at home for carrying out their work, with particular care given to ensuring proper ergonomics;

3.2.3 Are assisted in respect of risks to their mental health including stress and/or depression;

3.2.4 Have a suitable system in place for reporting accidents or injuries during working hours;

3.2.5 Are taking adequate breaks when they work from home;

3.2.6 Get regular contact and communication from their line and team management;

3.2.7 Working hours are not excessive.

4. STANDARD OPERATING PROCEDURES (SOP's)

WFH employees are referred to their line or team managers for SOP's for all duties previously conducted offline, and the aforementioned must be read in conjunction with this policy and procedure.

5. EMPLOYEE AVAILABILITY AND WORKING HOURS

5.1 Working hours and working arrangements

5.1.1 Employees are to work a standard 5-day, 45 hour work week. Individuals are to make use of [insert name of time-tracking software] to track the number of hours worked.

5.1.2 These hours can be clocked at any time of the day but not on weekends. However, employees need to be present every weekday between 8:00am and 8:30am, and do morning check-ins with their teams via [insert software] and remain available to respond immediately to calls and emails between 8:30 am to 17:00.

5.1.3 The lunch break time will be from 13h00 up to 14h00.

5.1.4 Team or Line Managers are to monitor the attendance of their teams and maintain a register. Should an employee be absent, this is to be recorded for actioning.

5.1.5 Daily tasks and output requirements will be saved on [software] and the same will be updated on an ongoing basis. Employees need to be responsive and energetic at all times to messages, emails and all liaisons and task related communications. Standards of output and the achievement of targets will be closely monitored, as will be absenteeism and absence from work stations.

5.1.6 The late joining of virtual meetings will not be tolerated and the EFH requirement is that meetings must be joined at least 5 (five) minutes before the start of the meeting, without exceptions.

5.1.7 To ensure that employee performance will not be detrimentally effected, employees are to:

- Elect and choose a distraction-free working space;
- Have an adequate internet connection;
- Dedicate their full attention to their job duties during working hours;
- Adhere to break and attendance schedules agreed upon with their manager;
- Ensure their schedules overlap with those of their team members for as long as is necessary to complete their duties effectively and productively.

Team members and managers should determine and distinguish between long-term and short-term goals. They should frequently meet (either online or in-person when possible) to discuss progress and results.

5.1.8 All terms and conditions of contracts of employment and letters of appointment continue to be in force, and employees must continue to comply with rules in respect of:

- Internet and IT rules and regulations;
- Attendance and absenteeism;
- Performance and achievement of targets;
- Discipline and employee code of conduct;
- Conduct off-company premises;
- Social media;
- Confidentiality and non-disclosure of information;
- Data protection and security;
- Dress code when meeting with customers, managers and fellow employees;
- Employer communication requirements and employee availability.

5.1.9 Protocols in respect of requests for annual leave, sick leave and all statutory leave entitlements, as well as requests for leave of absence, must be processed through line management and appropriate channels of communication.

6. SUPPORT MEASURES: EQUIPMENT AND TRAINING

6.1 It is the responsibility of the employer to ensure that appropriate equipment, systems, and technology to support remote working are properly installed, are functioning and maintained and that employees have the required training to operate those systems.

6.2 For digital work, the employer will ensure employees are aware of increased data protection and cyber security risks and will provide suitable software and training, to ensure the necessary understanding of and compliance with data protection policies.

6.3 Employees will be provided with any other necessary training to carry out their job effectively while working from home, at the discretion of the employer.

6.4 Equipment provided is and remains property of the employer. Employees have a duty to keep it safe and to avoid any misuse thereof. Specifically employees are required to:

- Keep their equipment password protected;
- Store equipment in a safe and clean space when not in use;
- Follow all data encryption, protection standard and settings;
- Refrain from downloading suspicious, unauthorized or illegal software;
- Comply with the employer's electronic mail/internet rules and regulations.

7. SURVEILLANCE AND PERFORMANCE MONITORING

The employer has the right to monitor the performance of duties of employees, conversely:

7.1 Employees will have access to, and influence over, data collected on themselves (if any);

7.2 Sustainable data processing safeguards will be implemented;

7.3 The "data minimalization principle" will be applied;

7.4 Data processing will be transparent;

7.5 Privacy and fundamental rights will be respected;

7.6 Biometric data and Personally Identifiable Information (PII) will be exempt from normal monitoring;

7.7 Surveillance in respect of the employees' location or whereabouts will not be used unless there is an intrinsic need for doing so.

8. WORK RELATED EXPENSES

8.1 Working from home will not lead to cost shifting from employers to WFH employees. The cost of both one-off and recurring expenses that the employer would normally be responsible for on employer provided premises, will remain the responsibility of the employer.

8.2 The employer will provide, as necessary and by agreement, an adequate allowance or full cost reimbursement for all work related expenses including water, electricity and gas, stationery, equipment, amenities, telephone, internet expenses and security.

8.3 The insurance cover in respect of the employer's equipment, will be for the account of the employer.

9. CONCLUSION

9.1 WFH can result in unintended negative, as well as unforeseen consequences, with a direct impact on the employment relationship.

9.2 Inevitably, WFH brings with it the increased risk of working life impinging on non-working life, and the encroachment of work into the personal domain and sphere of the employee. It is important that WFH occurs within legal and reasonable limits, on working time. Regulations and limits around working times serves as a fundamental protection for employees. This means that:

9.2.1 Flexible work arrangements must be based on agreement and good faith conduct;

9.2.2 Employees have a right to, conditionally, disconnect from work;

9.2.3 Employees will not be encouraged or rewarded for being constantly connected;

9.2.4 Records regarding employee working hours including breaks, starting and finishing times, must be kept and made available for inspection by a properly authorized person when required;

9.2.5 Generally, a collaborative management style must be implemented in order to achieve the purposes of this policy and procedure.

SAMPLE

ELECTRONICS COMMUNICATION AND DIGITAL POLICY

1. INTRODUCTION AND POLICY PURPOSE

1.1 The allocation and use of electronic communications to employees is intended as a productivity tool to aid and assist employees in the performance of their duties. Such communications include electronic mail, voicemail, instant messaging, text and SMS messages.

1.2 The Company's software and digital systems inclusive of the use of its electronic communication is to increase efficiency and effectiveness. Such communications are Company property and the sole purpose is to facilitate Company business.

1.3 Any attempt not to comply with the policy will constitute material breach of contract.

2. SCOPE

2.1 This policy applies to all employees, inclusive of WFH employees, and any users (remote and local) authorized to access the Company's email and internet system. This policy also applies to all electronic mail originating through the Company's email lists accessed through the use of the email system.

2.2 The words *"employer"* and *"company"* are used interchangeably in this document.

3. POLICY GUIDELINES

3.1 The Company makes its electronic mail/internet system available to employees for conducting official business, and in the furtherance of Company business efficiency. The following must be noted:

- The use of the system is a privilege, not a right;
- The records including all email and logs through the use of this system are the property of the Company and not of the employee;
- The Company reserves the right to monitor the operation of this system, and employees have been advised of this fact.

3.2 In respect of general employee privacy, the policy is as follows:

3.2.1 The Company in principle respects the privacy and dignity of all individuals. Access is limited to personal information to authorized personnel who need it for business or legal purposes and the employer will comply within reason, with all applicable laws regarding disclosure of personal information.

3.2.2 The employer does not routinely monitor personal communications and computer use of its employees, nor search their work spaces. The employee should not, however, expect that these communications and work spaces will be private and the company may elect to monitor such communications and/or search work spaces. There may be times when appropriate Company personnel may access employee work spaces and monitor electronic and other communications for the safety or protection of other people, Company property or other reasons. Employees are not permitted to access the electronic communications of other employees or third parties unless directed to do so by the employer.

3.2.3 The employer uses various forms of electronic communications including, but not limited to, computers, e-mail, telephones, voicemail, and other software. All electronic communications, including all software and hardware, are the sole property of the employer and are to be used only for Company business.

3.2.4 Electronic communication/media may not be used in any manner that would be discriminatory, harassing or obscene, or for any other purpose which is illegal, against company policy or not in the best interest of the employer.

3.2.5 Employees who misuse electronic communications and engage in defamation, copyright or trademark infringement, misappropriation of trade secrets, discrimination, harassment or related actions will be subject to disciplinary action, and dismissal.

4. RULES OF ELECTRONIC COMMUNICATION

4.1 **Authorized Usage**: The electronic communication systems must be used solely to facilitate the business of the employer. Employees are prohibited from using electronic communication systems for private business activities, personal or for amusement purposes.

4.2 Accordingly, employees are strictly prohibited from using the employer's own computers, e-mail systems and internet access accounts for personal reasons or for any improper purpose. Some specific examples of prohibited uses include, but are not limited to:

4.2.1 Transmitting, retrieving, downloading, or storing messages or images that are offensive, derogatory, off colour, sexual in content, or otherwise inappropriate in a business environment.

4.2.2 Making threatening or harassing statements to another employee or to a vendor, customer or other outside party.
4.2.3 Transmitting, retrieving, downloading, or storing messages or images related to race, religion, colour, sex, national origin, citizenship status, age, handicap, disability, sexual orientation, or any other status protected under federal, state and local laws.
4.2.4 Communicating confidential employer information to individuals inside or outside the company or to other organisations, without specific authorization from management to do so.
4.2.5 Sending or receiving confidential or copyrighted materials without prior authorization.
4.2.6 Soliciting personal business opportunities, or personal advertising.
4.2.7 Gambling, monitoring sports scores, or playing electronic games.
4.2.8 Irrespective of the circumstances, individual passwords must never be shared or revealed to anyone else besides the authorized user.
4.2.9 Misrepresenting, obscuring, suppressing, or replacing a user's identity on an electronic communications system is forbidden. The user name, electronic mail address, organisational affiliation, and related information included with electronic messages or postings must reflect the actual originator of the messages or postings.

4.3 **Contents of Messages**: The use of profanity, obscenities or derogatory remarks in electronic messages is strictly prohibited. Special caution is warranted because backup and archival copies of electronic mail may actually be more permanent and more readily accessed than traditional paper communications. Therefore, transmission of obscene, harassing or otherwise inappropriate messages is strictly prohibited.

4.4 **Copyright Issues:** Copyright materials belonging to entities other than this Company, may not be transmitted by employees on the Company's email/internet system. All employees, obtaining access to other companies' or individuals' materials must respect all copyrights and may not copy, retrieve, modify or forward copyrighted materials, except with permission, or as a single copy to reference only. Failure to observe copyright or license agreements may result in disciplinary action, and dismissal.

4.5 **Email Disclaimer:** The official email disclaimer (below) should always appear at the bottom of all email messages sent out by the Company's employees:

4.6 "DISCLAIMER: The information in this message is confidential and may be legally privileged. It is intended solely for the addressee. Access to this message by anyone else unauthorized. IF you are not the intended recipient, any disclosure, copying, or distribution of the message, or any action or omission taken by your in reliance on it, is prohibited and may be unlawful. Please immediately contact the sender if you have received in error. Thank you."

4.7 **No Expectation of Privacy:** Employees should expect that all information created, transmitted, downloaded, received or stored in the employer's computers, or other electronic devices may be accessed by the company at any time, without prior notice. Employees should not assume that they have an expectation of privacy or confidentiality in such messages or information (whether or not such messages or information is password protected), or that deleted messages are necessarily removed from the system.

5. SECURITY AND MESSAGE MONITORING

5.1 The Company routinely monitors usage patterns for its email/internet communications. The reasons for such are numerous, including cost analysis/allocation and the management of the Company's gateway to the internet. All messages created, sent or retrieved over the Company's email/internet are the property of the Company and should be considered public information. The Employer reserves the right to access and monitor all messages and files on the Company's email/internet system.

5.2 Accordingly, contents of electronic communications and the usage of electronic communications systems will be monitored to support operational, maintenance, auditing, security and investigative activities. The Company reserves the right to disclose any electronic messages to law enforcement officials without prior notice to any employee who may have sent or received such messages. Employees should structure their electronic communications in recognition of the fact that employers will, from time to time, examine the content of electronic communications. Employees are reminded that all messages are Company records. Therefore, the employer, reserves the right to access and disclose all messages sent over its electronic messaging systems or stored on its computers and electronic devices.

5.3 Employees are obliged to promptly report all information inclusive of security alerts, warnings, and suspected vulnerabilities, to management. Employees are also encouraged to promptly report any offensive electronic mail messages, telephone calls, and/or other communication to their immediate manager.

6. MONITORING OF EMPLOYEE ACTIVITIES AT WORK, REMOTELY AND AT THE WFH OFFICE

6.1 The Constitutional right to privacy, inclusive of the right not to have the privacy of communications infringed, is not an absolute right and all rights may be limited in accordance with section 36 of the Constitution.

6.2 It is generally accepted that the employee's right to privacy must be balanced and interpreted in the light of the Company's business interests, necessities or operational requirements. The employer has the right to control the working life of the employee, in accordance with the contract of employment's terms and conditions.

6.3 The Company recognizes that the monitoring of employee's activities in the workplace, as well as remotely (inclusive of the WFH office) electronically or by any other means, is a sensitive issue. The employee's right to privacy must be interpreted in the light of the employer's right to monitor employees to protect the business from abuse, (and possible extinction) to prevent criminal activity and to ensure health and safety of all concerned.

6.4 The employer only intends to engage in electronic monitoring and surveillance, if there is a legitimate reason for such surveillance to take place, and with due regard to all of the prevailing circumstances.

6.5 Any and all data collected by the Company through electronic surveillance devices shall be used for safety, security, health, employment relations and contract of employment compliances and adherences by employers. Electronic surveillance equipment is not for the purpose of invading the legitimate privacy of employees, nor to "spy" on employees but for valid operational and business reasons.

7. CONCLUSION

7.1 The fourth industrial revolution will make increased demands on the employer and its employees to abide by and to comply with rules, protocols and legislation in respect of data usage, storage and electronic communication systems.

7.2 Transparency, honesty and good faith conduct by both employer and employee, in respect of non-confidential matters, is of paramount importance and breaches of contract will not be tolerated.

7.3 This policy and procedure is subject to change and/or amendments as a result of statutory developments.

SAMPLE

RETIREMENT POLICY AND PROCEDURE

1. INTRODUCTION

1.1 The Employer's Retirement Policy consists of a mandatory retirement at the age of ____________ (state retirement age), and such policy condition has been previously communicated and/or agreed with employees.

1.2 The Employer's standard contract of employment retirement age provision states as follows:

1.3 *"The parties specifically agree that the normal retirement is at _____ years of age. The employee's service shall for this reason automatically terminates at the end of the year in which he/she reaches the agreed retirement age."*

AND

1.4 *"In terms of Company Policy having reached the mandatory retirement age of ______ will constitute a termination by operation of law and same will not constitute a dismissal. The Company has a discretion to allow any employee to work beyond the age of _____ and each retiree will be treated on individual merit and circumstances."* (**this is an optional clause**)

1.5 It is also recorded that Section 187 (2)(b) of the LRA states as follows:

1.6 "(b) a dismissal based on age is fair it the employee has reached the normal or agreed retirement age for persons employed in that capacity."

2. INTENTION AND PURPOSE

2.1 To determine the Employer's retirement age policy, and to provide for a procedure (which is not inflexible and could be customized for individual circumstances) to regulate the retirement of employees.

2.2 To give effect to Retirement and/or Provident Fund membership terms and conditions, if applicable.

2.3 Principles and Procedure

2.3.1 **Retirement**

This is normal retirement whereby the employment contract ends at the end of the month in which the employee turns _____ as stipulated in this policy.

2.3.2 **Early Retirement**

Early retirement arises when an employee applies for retirement before the year in which he/she turns ____ (age). An employee may elect to retire at any time after attaining the age of 55 years, provided that he/she gives the required notice and subject to approval. At the age of 55 the normal early retirement process will be initiated including the commencement of retirement benefits in terms of the Fund rules (if any).

2.3.3 **Appointment Post Retirement**

2.3.3.1 The appointment of an individual after the age of ____ (age) will not normally be possible but may be approved subject to certain conditions, for instance, in order to complete a specific project or phase of work.

2.3.3.2 The re-appointment of an individual after early retirement is also possible, subject to the employer's discretion.

2.3.4 **Retiree Exit**

The retirement process will normally be subject to a process of consultation which could be initiated either by the retiree or the employer, in order to clarify possible outstanding employment issues.

SAMPLE

REMUNERATION AND INCENTIVE SCHEME GUIDELINES

1. INTRODUCTION

1.1 The traditional method of remunerating employees in South Africa consists of (a) across the board (CPI and inflation linked) increases and (b) individual *"merit increases"* based on annual performance assessments, and (c) an annual *"bonus"* or *"13th cheque"*, either guaranteed or dependent on Company performance and profitability". Some employees are also paid commissions on the sale of goods and/or the achievement of stated targets.

1.2 The employer intends to continue to attract and to compete for top talent in order to assist the Company to thrive towards a competitive and successful future. This means the regular revision and if necessary updating of existing remuneration practices and policies.

1.3 "Revision" may not always be consistent with the offering of higher salaries, but may involve reducing fixed pay, while increasing variable pay, that is directly linked to employee performance and productivity. This will assist to incentivize employees to perform at a higher level, while maintaining a healthy and competitive environment.

2. GUIDELINE BRIEF AND OBJECTIVES

2.1 These guidelines are intended to provide for a framework and guidance for the consideration of alternative methods of remuneration, in order to ensure that the employer remains competitive, profitable as well as best prepared to meet the demands of customers.

2.2 "Incentivized pay" provides for a powerful tool to focus employees on (a) their immediate goal to earn a substantial amount of money, (b) by achieving the targets set by the Company.

3. ELEMENTS OF REMUNERATION *"PACKAGES"*

3.1 For the purposes of this policy, the following forms of remuneration can be distinguished, i.e.:

3.1.1 Basic Pay – the basic (gross) wage or salary

3.1.2 Annual Bonuses – or discretionary bonuses – the 13th cheque

3.1.3 Incentive Pay – a bonus paid (normally as a commission) when specified performance objectives are met and payable by agreement or the achievement of targets

3.1.4 Commission Earnings - a form of remuneration and/or salary directly linked to the number of items sold on a percentage of overall income achieved for the employer.

3.2 Setting pay levels

3.2.1 Basic pay and salary levels are normally set as a result of comparative and competitor salaries, as well as the inherent value of the job - determined by scarcity and key-skills.

3.2.2 "Unconventional pay systems" must be considered and introduced, as a way to reduce fixed monthly overheads, to save costs, and to pass this on to employees through revised remuneration systems.

3.1 Individual Merit, "pay for" Performance Program

3.1.1 *"Pay-for-Performance"* ties pay directly to an individual's performance in meeting specified business targets. The targets have accompanying metrics that makes it possible to track performance. The metrics can be financial indicators, or they can be indirect indicators such as customer satisfaction or work progress. *"Pay-for-Performance"* schemes often combine a fixed basic salary with a valuable pay component, e.g., bonuses.

3.1.2 The more traditional merit pay increase refers to an increase to an employee's base pay due to high performance. These raises are typically delivered on an annual basis, and are budgeted for as part of the annual salary increase budgeting process. Merit pay increases are the most commonly used pay-for-performance model for recognition of employee performance, as they deferentially reward top performers for their contributions with a bump to their base salary for the following year.

3.2 Variable Pay Programs and Team Bonuses

3.2.1 Variable pay programs encompass a variety of discretionary and non-discretionary bonuses that can vary according to the pay out period, the employees who are eligible, and the metrics that employees are measured against. Unlike merit pay increases, variable pay programs are increasingly administered not just annually but multiple times a year (e.g., once a quarter) and a mix of different variable pay programs are often used in combination to achieve the desired results.

3.2.2 **Discretionary bonuses** are individually geared and orientated, and awarded on an *ad-hoc* basis to employees who demonstrate exceptional performance, often without consideration for pre-defined goals and objectives. Some common discretionary bonus types are:

3.2.2.1 **Spot bonuses** - Reward employees *"on the spot"* for achievements that deserve special recognition.

3.2.2.2 **Project bonuses -** Reward employees for completion or expedited completion of a specific project.

3.2.2.3 **Retention bonuses -** Typically awarded to key positions and critical skills employees, in order to decrease the flight risk of such key personnel.

3.2.3 **Non-discretionary bonuses** are awarded when employees, teams, or the entire Company meets specific, pre-defined targets. Based on the duration of the assessment period (the amount of time over which performance is measured), they are considered either short-term incentives or long-term incentives. Non-discretionary bonuses include:

3.2.3.1 **Company-wide bonuses** - these focus around specific improvement goals or *"sacrificial"* goals for the organization and reward employees based on goal achievement.

3.2.3.2 **Team-incentive bonuses** - these focus around specific achievement or improvement goals for one team (e.g., marketing or sales).

3.2.3.3 **Individual incentive bonuses** - based on predetermined, measurable business objectives that are evaluated periodically (e.g., each quarter) based on one person's performance, but could also be based on the achievement of a specific target.

4. CONCLUSION - COMPENSATION LINKED TO PERFORMANCE

4.1 In order to secure and to retain scarce skills, employers will have little option but to boost employee engagement, through compensation and performance target achievement systems.

4.2 It is acknowledged that:

4.2.1 Properly and professionally introduced pay-for-performance models, geared towards the individual employee and to improve employee engagement and retention, by clearly tying employee or Company achievement of performance targets to tangible financial rewards. These programs also enable employees to see a direct connection between the work they do every day and the success of the enterprise as a whole.

4.2.2 Since employees are more frequently awarded, more regular conversations are facilitated about individual and Company performance, allowing managers to provide critical feedback outside of the annual review process.

4.2.3 Pay-for-performance plans can help employees grow exponentially due to the inherent desire to be rewarded. Frequent rewards can also lead to increased employee retention, as the motivation of money assists to keep staff. It has been established that increased retention is beneficial to the enterprise and lead to greater productivity and lower turnover costs.

SAMPLE

MATERNITY AND PATERNITY POLICY AND PROCEDURE

1. **PURPOSE AND SCOPE**

    1.1 The purpose of this policy and procedure is to set out the procedure applicable to defined employees who are entitled to the statutory provisions of the Basic Conditions of Employment Act (the *"BCEA"*).

    1.2 The principles regarding maternity as well as paternity leave contained in the BCEA, or any applicable Collective Bargaining Agreement, will apply.

2. **MATERNITY LEAVE**

    2.1 All female employees are entitled to maternity leave; as provided for in statute.

    2.2 Employees that qualify for maternity leave are entitled to submit an application for benefits to the Unemployment Insurance Fund (UIF) Claims Officer, in the matter prescribed in the UIF Act, who will then determine if the employee is entitled to receive UIF compensation.

    2.3 The following maternity leave and employee rights before, during and after confinement are applicable:

        2.3.1 A pregnant employee is entitled to 4 (four) consecutive month's paid maternity leave.

        2.3.2 An employee may commence such leave any time from 4 (four) weeks before the expected date of birth, unless otherwise agreed; or

        2.3.3 On a date from which a medical practitioner or midwife certifies that it is necessary for the employee's health or that of her unborn child.

        2.3.4 No employee may resume work during the 6 (six) weeks after the birth of her child, unless a medical practitioner or midwife certifies that she is fit to do so.

        2.3.5 An employee must notify her employer in writing, unless the employee is unable to do so, of the date on which she intends to:

            2.3.5.1 Commence maternity leave; and

            2.3.5.2 Return to work after maternity leave.

        2.3.6 Notification must be given:

            2.3.6.1 At least 8 (eight) weeks before the employee intends to commence maternity leave.

2.3.7 No employer may require or permit a pregnant employee or an employee who is nursing a child to perform work that is hazardous to her health or the health of her child.

2.4 The following guidelines are applicable for maternity benefits

2.4.1 Annual leave will accrue during the first four months of maternity leave.

2.4.2 The employer will assist the employee, if requested to do so, to file claims with the UIF and will provide her with the necessary claim information and documentation.

3. PATERNITY LEAVE

3.1 An employee who is a parent of a child will be entitled to 10 (ten) paid consecutive days' parental leave. This applies irrespective of the gender, which means it would include parents in same sex relationships. Note must be taken of the comparative benefits, i.e., (a) for mothers who give birth (maternity leave), (b) parental leave, (c) a person who adopts a child (adoption leave) or (d) a commissioning parent in a surrogate motherhood agreement (commissioning parental leave).

3.2 Parental leave may commence on the day that the child is born. The 10 (ten) consecutive days parental leave are considered as calendar days, not working days.

3.3 In respect of adoption leave – (10 consecutive weeks), this relates to the adoption of a child that is below the age of 1 (two) years of age, as follows:

3.4 a single adoptive parent is entitled to 10 (ten) consecutive weeks' adoption leave. If there are two adoptive parents, only one would be entitled to the 10 (ten) consecutive weeks' adoption leave. However, the other adoptive parent would be entitled to 10 (ten) consecutive days' normal parental leave and the adoptive parents must decide who will be taking adoption leave, and who will be taking normal parental leave.

NOTE:

Leave may commence on the day that the adoption order is granted or the day that a competent court places the child in the care of a prospective parent.

3.5 In respect of *"commissioning parental leave"* – (10 consecutive weeks), this category of leave relates to surrogate motherhood. The commissioning parent will primarily be responsible for caring for the child (primary commissioning parent) will be entitled to commissioning parental leave.

3.6 The employer must be notified by the employee, which notification requires that:

  3.6.1 the employee must give at least 1 (one) month's written notice of:

    3.6.1.1 the expected date of birth, as well as when the leave is due to commence and when the employee will return to work; or

    3.6.1.2 in the case of adoption, the date on which adoption order is granted or the day that a competent court places the child in the care of a prospective adoptive parent.

3.7 The employer reserves the right in respect of employees that fail and/or refuse and/or reject to comply with such notification requirement, not to allow such employee to proceed on the leave concerned.

3.8 Unemployment insurance benefits are available to persons in the abovementioned categories.

SAMPLE POLICY

ABSENTEEISM MANAGEMENT POLICY AND PROCEDURE

1. **INTRODUCTION**

1.1 All employees have a basic contractual duty to report for work on time, to perform work and not to leave work without permission.

1.2 Unauthorized absenteeism comes at an enormous cost to the Company and will not be tolerated. Such conduct could also constitute material breach of contract.

1.3 "Absenteeism", for the purposes of this policy, is absence from the workplace without permission ("AWOP"). This policy and procedure provides for a guideline to deal with unauthorized absence, poorly explained absence, and AWOP.

1.4 The basic rule is that should an employee be unable to report for duty due to unforeseen circumstances, the employee has the obligation to inform his immediate manager before 10h00 on the first day of absence.

1.5 The Company is committed to stamping out unauthorised absenteeism by ensuring all culpable incidents are investigated and actioned timeously, where appropriate. Managers are to make sure all incidents of unauthorized absence are followed up by a post-absence interview; and that the requisite documentation is completed and submitted for record keeping purposes.

1.6 The arrangement and conduct of such post-absenteeism interviews provides for the foundation of this entire policy and procedure, is intended to rehabilitate transgressors and in order to prevent a poor Company attendance record.

1.7 All employees must provide the Company with the exact and correct contact and residential details, and have the duty to keep the Company informed of changes of contact details.

1.8 If an employee has been absent from duty for a period of 5 (five) continuous days, such employee is deemed to have absconded or deserted.

2. **DEFINITIONS**

2.1 "Absenteeism" ("AWOP") means the absence from work without permission.

2.2 "Desertion" means that the employee has abandoned the Employer with no intention of returning to the Company's employment, for instance, by taking up employment elsewhere.

2.3 "Abscondment" is deemed to have occurred when the employee is absent from work for a time that warrants the inference that the employee cannot or does not intend to return to work, for whatever reason.

2.4 "Culpable Absenteeism" means unauthorized absenteeism where the employee is blameworthy and guilty of misconduct.

2.5 "Innocent Absenteeism" means an employee who takes statutory leave or leave with permission.

2.6 "Incapacity" means the employee suffers from ill-health and/or is not in a position to comply with contractual obligations for reasons beyond the control of such employee.

2.7 "Company" or "Employer" refers to the same legal entity.

3. ABSENTEEISM POLICY

3.1 Employees whose work attendance records are unsatisfactory through habitual lateness, unauthorised absence or persistent absence are liable to have disciplinary action taken against them which could include dismissal. This also constitutes material breach of contract, as well as a threat to the job security of fellow employees.

3.2 The Company's disciplinary policy in respect of absence without permission (AWOP) and related timekeeping offences, is one of **zero tolerance** (within reason and the principles of fairness) and is classified as a category 1 (one) offence which could lead to summary dismissal as a result of gross as well as material breach of contract (see attached AWOP Disciplinary Code).

3.3 The Company reserves the right to question and scrutinize all sick certificates and/or to reject the same, especially in the event of suspicious circumstances.

3.4 There is a limited obligation on the Employer to establish the whereabouts of the missing employee, and management will endeavour to make telephone and/or other contact in order to find such employee, with due regard to the circumstances of each individual case.

3.5 Absence will also be regarded as unauthorised if any employee fails to report for work the day before or after a weekend, pay weekend or paid public holiday, or long weekend, without good reason.

3.6 Periods of recurring absence, even where there has been full compliance with Company sickness-absence notification and certification requirements, can still be viewed by the Company as a problematic matter which could result in dismissal on the basis of incapacity.

3.7 Employees are required to remain at work until the normal finishing time. Unauthorised early leaving is regarding as a serious offence.

3.8 The provisions of this policy and procedure must be read in conjunction with Schedule 8 to the LRA, a Code of Good Practice: Dismissal.

4. ABUSE OF SICK LEAVE

4.1 In terms of statutory provisions the employee is entitled to, during the first 6 (six) months of employment, 1 (one) day's paid sick leave for every 26 (twenty-six) days worked. After a period of 6 (six) months, the employee will be entitled to 30 (thirty) days sick leave over a sick leave cycle of 36 (thirty-six) months.

4.2 Should the employee be unable to attend work because of illness, the employee is required to notify his/her line manager before 10h00 on that day.

4.3 The Company is not required to pay the employee sick leave in the event of:

4.3.1 The employee being absent from work for more than 2 (two) consecutive days; and/or

4.3.2 The employee being absent from work on more than 2 (two) occasions during an 8 (eight) week period; and/or

4.3.3 The employee being absent from work on the day before and/or the day after a long weekend or a paid public holiday; and/or

4.3.4 On request by the Employer, failure by the employee to produce a medical certificate stating that he or she was unable to work for the duration of his or her absence on account of sickness or injury, and/or

4.3.5 The employee abusing sick leave provisions.

4.4 Defective sick notes will be rejected and the principle of no-work no-pay will apply. A sick note must comply with the following:

4.4.1 The name and the qualification of the person issuing the certificate;

4.4.2 A contact number and physical address;

4.4.3 A proper practice or registration number;

4.4.4 A short description of the medical problem. (The medical practitioner does not have to give a detailed diagnosis because of doctor/patient privilege).

4.4.5 The date of the examination;

4.4.6 The signature of the practitioner;

4.4.7 Be an original document;

4.4.8 Must be legible.

5. PROCEDURES

5.1 In all cases of absence the employee is required to contact immediate management directly, by no later than 10h00 on the (first) day of absence, in order to advise on:

5.1.1 Reason(s) for AWOP;

5.1.2 Expected duration of absence.

5.1.3 The employee bears the onus to prove that he had in fact communicated with management.

5.2 AWOP employees are required to report to immediate management upon their return in order to undergo a post AWOP interview which will be documented.

5.3 Bona fide absentees may be required to complete an application for leave form.

5.4 The principle of no-work no-pay applies to the provisions of this policy.

5.5 Employees who are in breach of the provisions of this policy will be subject to appropriate discipline (see attached disciplinary code). Sanctions could range from warnings to dismissal, depending on the severity of the absenteeism and the number of previous warnings, if any.

5.6 Absent employees who have been in breach of the 5 (five) day period of grace referred to in clause 1.8 hereto, are considered to have absconded or deserted under such circumstances.

AWOP DISCIPLINARY CODE AND GUIDELINE

Nature of Transgression	Offence	Sanction
1. Leaving Company premises while on duty without permission.	1st Offence	Dismissal
2. Absent from work for more than 2 (two) consecutive working days without complying with the Company Policies and Procedures, and/or failing to report absence to the Company at the earliest possible opportunity.	1st Offence 2nd Offence	Written warning Dismissal
3. Absence on the day before the commencement of a weekend or public holiday or on the day thereafter.	1st Offence	Dismissal
4. Falsification of records and/or documentation, e.g., timesheets.	1st Offence	Dismissal

Nature of Transgression	Offence	Sanction
5. Changing a medical certificate or using a false one.	1st Offence	Dismissal
6. Desertion or abscondment/absence for more than 5 days.	1st Offence	Breach of contract termination/Employer acceptance of repudiation of contract
7. Impairment and/or destruction of trust relationship through abuse of sick leave, fraud and dishonesty.	1st Offence	Dismissal
8. Any AWOP dishonesty or attempted dishonestly inclusive of misrepresentation, false or misleading statement and/or sick leave abuse	1st Offence	Dismissal
9. Absence for 1 (one) working day without a valid reason	1st Offence 2nd Offence 3rd Offence	Written warning Final written warning Dismissal
10. Poor timekeeping or being late for work and/or failing to inform management on a day of absence before 10h00	1st Offence 2nd Offence 3rd Offence	Written warning Final written warning Dismissal
11. Failing to report for overtime work when agreed to do so	1st Offence 2nd Offence	Final written warning Dismissal
12. Failing to produce a medical certificate when requested to do so.	1st Offence 2nd Offence 3rd Offence	Written warning Final written warning Dismissal

SAMPLE

POOR WORK PERFORMANCE POLICY AND PROCEDURE

1. INTRODUCTION

1.1 A contract of employment may be terminated for one, all or some of the following valid reasons, i.e.:

1.1.1 Misconduct/Behaviour

1.1.2 Inability/Capacity/Incompetence

1.1.3 Retrenchment/Redundancy

1.2 This Policy is concerned with poor performance management and Schedule 8 – Code of Good Practice: Dismissal (Item 9) must be read as an inextricable part of this Policy. Item 9 is stated as follows:

*"**9 Guidelines in cases of dismissal for poor work performance***
Any person determining whether a dismissal for poor work performance is unfair should consider –

(a) *Whether or not the employee failed to meet a performance standard; and*

(b) *If the employee did not meet a required performance standard whether or not –*

(i) the employee was aware, or could reasonably be expected to have been aware, of the required performance standard;

(ii) the employee was given a fair opportunity to meet the required performance standard; and

(iii) dismissal was an appropriate sanction for not meeting the required performance standard."

1.2.1 It is the intention as well as objectives of this Procedure to draw a clear distinction between the termination of services on a *"no fault"* basis, i.e., as a result of incapacity and/or inability to perform duties, as distinct from misconduct and behaviour-related transgressions where the employee clearly is at fault.

1.2.2 Evaluations in respect of the capacity and/or ability to perform in accordance with laid down standards, will be entirely at the discretion of the Company's management, and in accordance with the guidelines of the Code of Good Practice (see above).

1.2.3 This Policy and Procedure will be applicable in the event of incapacity, incompetence, under-performance as well as breaches of contract over which the employee has no control.

1.1 This Policy and Procedure will be implemented by management when it becomes necessary to counsel the employee on poor work performance.

1.2.4 Incapacity (not for medical incapacity);

1.2.5 Failure to perform duties in accordance with established standards;

1.2.6 Incompetence; and

1.2.7 Poor performance as a result of inability to achieve and/or meet standards.

2. OBJECTIVES

The objectives of this Policy and Procedure (read with the Code of Good Practice) are as follows, to:

2.1 To identify situations of incapacity and/or inability to perform and to take such actions as may be necessary in the interest of the Company, as well as the interest of the employee.

2.2 Evaluate such situation timeously and rationally.

2.3 Comply with the standards of substantive and procedural fairness.

2.4 Terminate services of employment on a fair and rational basis, on the basis of capacity and/or ability to perform, at the discretion of management.

3. DEFINITIONS

3.1 "Misconduct" is defined as improper conduct, unacceptable behaviour, as well as deliberate act or acts in contravention of standards, rules and regulations.

3.2 "Incapacity" or "Incompetence" means the ability to carry out instructions and/or to work as a result of physical and/or mental conditions.

3.3 "Medical incapacity" means an inability to comply as a result of illness and/or medical conditions that prevent and/or interferes with contractual obligations.

3.4 "Performance" means the effective execution of instructions; the carrying out of instructions and duties; achievement under test and achieving standards set.

3.5 "Poor Performance" means an employee's ability to reach targets or to comply with the Company's expected standards of performance. An employee who is not attaining the required results or achieving the performance targets set for him (in absence of deliberate poor performance, which will constitute misconduct) is not, in the first instance, guilty of a disciplinary offence - as is the case with an act of misconduct - and counselling should be given to assist the employee in overcoming problems experienced. The Company may terminate the employment contract if the individual fails to meet the required standard of performance.

3.6 "Negligence" means a lack of proper care of attention; carelessness.

4. PROCEDURES AND GUIDELINES

4.1 Introduction

Standards and targets are established and set by the employer and forms part and parcel of contracts of employment.

Performance will normally be measured by:

- Achievement of set or agreed standards
- Sales targets/outputs/completion of tasks
- Sales activities and call reports (if applicable)
- Time taken to achieve results
- Customer surveys
- Result against targets
- Appraisal interviews

[In respect of sales staff the Compensation Plan provided for elsewhere as a contractual provision must be read as an integral part of these procedures (optional).]

4.2 In respect of medical incapacity item 10 and 11 of the Code of Good Conduct - Dismissal shall be applicable.

Step 1 - Preparatory Action

- Conduct a preliminary investigation/evaluation
- Establish:
  - The employee's contractual responsibilities and performance targets;
  - Whether he has been trained and guide at this job (if necessary);
  - Measure of performance in respect of quality, time to complete a job, quantity, etc.
  - Is there full compliance with employment duties?
  - Degree (if any) of loss of confidence in employee's abilities, efficiency and/or competence.

Step 2 - Counselling the Employee

- Meet with employee and counsel the employee
- Establish:
  - Whether the employee is aware of the Company Policy on Performance

  - Whether he knows the Company's standards
  - Whether he knows the Company's expectations of him/her
  - Whether there is a task interference, i.e., does he have poor equipment
  - Whether he/she has any motivational problems or worries

  Thereafter, explain to the employee precisely what is expected in the future and take the necessary steps to train, supervise, guide, etc.

  - Identify, reiterate and refresh expectations
  - Continue to communicate performance standards and requirements clearly and unambiguously to the employee
  - Record the discussion and outcome in writing in a subsequent letter to the employee, with a follow-up date to appraise the employee's performance.
  - Should the employee's performance not improve significantly within an appropriate period, move to the next step.

Step 3 - Review Session

- Conduct a counselling session with the employee, with the following agenda:

  - Confirm, record of poor performance
  - Reiterate proper standards
  - Record the discussion and outcome in writing in a subsequent letter to the employee.

- The employee should be given a notification that his continued employment could be at risk if his poor performance continues.

Step 4 - Enquiry and Final Evaluation

- Should the situation not improve, then arrange for a formal enquiry in order to formally assess the situation. The main function of the enquiry will be to consider the circumstances and to decide whether the employee's services should be terminated or whether the employment relationship should be allowed to continue.
- Evaluate degree of loss of confidence in the employee's abilities, efficiency and/or competence.

SAMPLE POLICY

DISCIPLINARY CODE - SCHEDULE OF TRANSGRESSIONS AND PROPOSED SANCTIONS - A GUIDELINE

(To be read with items 1 to 4 of the LRA's Code of Good Conduct - Dismissal)

CATEGORY 1	**Disciplinary Hearing** **Possibility of Dismissal**		
CATEGORY 2	**Written Warning(s)**	**Disciplinary Hearing** **Possibility of Dismissal**	
CATEGORY 3	**Verbal Warning(s)**	**Written Warning(s)**	**Disciplinary Hearing** **Possibility of Dismissal**

NATURE OF TRANSGRESSION	FIRST TRANS-GRESSION	SECOND TRANS-GRESSION	THIRD TRANS-GRESSION
CATEGORY 1: GROSS MISCONDUCT/MATERIAL BREACH OF CONTRACT 1. Serious safety transgressions/ Non-compliance with health directives 2. Absence without permission (AWOP) 3. Refusal to obey or carry out instructions 4. Dishonesty/fraudulent and/or devious conduct a. Stealing or attempting to steal property belonging to either an employee or to the Company/unauthorized possession of property; b. Bribery or corruption; giving or receiving or attempting to give or receive any bribe or inducing or attempting to induce any person to perform any corrupt act c. False evidence; deliberately giving untrue, erroneous or misleading information or testimony whether verbally or in writing d. Forgery; falsifying or changing any document with fraudulent intent or attempting to do so e. Unauthorised disclosure of information to outside organisations inclusive of competitors f. Bad faith conduct g. Acting against the interest of the Company	**Disciplinary Hearing/ Possibility of Dismissal**		

NATURE OF TRANSGRESSION	FIRST TRANS-GRESSION	SECOND TRANS-GRESSION	THIRD TRANS-GRESSION
h. Bringing the name of the Company into disrepute i. Performing private work without permission 5. Poor work performance/gross inefficiency 6. Disrespectful/insulting conduct/defiance 7. Participation in unprocedural strike action and/or go-slows 8. Being in possession of a dangerous weapon without the Company's permission 9. Sexual harassment (in all forms) 10. Failure to work agreed overtime or undertake agreed extra duties where these are necessary and within legal limitations 11. Undermining the authority of management 12. Possession or use of illegal drugs 13. Possession of alcoholic beverages without managerial authority 14. The alleged commitment and/or participation in any criminal act 15. Damage to Company property 16. Abuse of sick leave 17. Physical violence or assault			
This schedule is not inflexible and provides for guidance only and management may, at its discretion, implement less or more severe disciplinary action as and when required. It is also not intended to provide for an exhaustive list of all possible transgressions nor penalties provided.			

SAMPLE

MEDICAL INCAPACITY POLICY AND PROCEDURE

1. INTRODUCTION

1.1 A contract of employment may be terminated for one, all or some of the following valid reasons, i.e.:

1.1.1 Misconduct/Behaviour

1.1.2 Inability/Capacity

1.1.3 Retrenchment/Redundancy

The LRA's Schedule 8 A Code of Good Practice – Dismissal states as follows:

"10 Incapacity: Ill Health and Injury

(1) *Incapacity on the grounds of ill health or injury may be temporary or permanent. If an employee is temporarily unable to work in these circumstances, the employer should investigate the extent of the incapacity or the injury. If the employee is likely to be absent for a time that is unreasonably long in the circumstances, the employer should investigate all the possible alternatives short of dismissal. When alternatives are considered, relevant factors might include the nature of the job, the period of absence, the seriousness of the illness or injury and the possibility of secreting a temporary replacement for the ill or injured employee. In cases of permanent incapacity, the employer should ascertain the possibility of securing alternative employment, or adapting the duties or work circumstances of the employees to accommodate the employee's disability.*

(2) *In the process of the investigation referred to in subsection (1) the employee should be allowed the opportunity to state a case in response and to be assisted by a trade union representative or fellow employee.*

(3) *The degree of incapacity is relevant to the fairness of any dismissal. The cause of the incapacity may also be relevant. In the case of certain kinds of incapacity, for example alcoholism or drug abuse, counselling and rehabilitation may be appropriate steps for an employer to consider.*

(4) *Particular consideration should be given to employees who are injured at work or who are incapacitated by work-related illness. The courts have indicated that the duty on the employer to accommodate the incapacity of the employee is more onerous in these circumstances.*

11 Guidelines in cases of dismissal arising from ill health or injury

Any person determining whether a dismissal arising from ill health or injury is unfair should consider -

(a) *whether or not the employee is capable of performing the work; and*

(b) *if the employee is not capable -*

   (i) the extent to which the employee is able to perform the work;

   (ii) the extent to which the employee's work circumstances might be adapted to accommodate disability, or, where this is not possible, the extent to which the employee's duties might be adapted; and

   (iii) the availability of any suitable alternative work."

2. POLICY, PROCEDURES AND GUIDELINES

2.1 This policy and procedure will be applicable in cases of employees not being able to perform duties satisfactorily as a result of sickness or ill-health.

2.2 Items 10 and 11 of the Code herein above have reference and will be used as a guideline to assess incapacity situations.

2.3 This policy and procedure supports the principle of identifying temporary ill-health from longer term permanent illnesses, with the assistance of medical opinion.

2.4 The objective difficulty or impossibility, of the employee to comply with duties as a result of medical incapacity, constitutes a breach of contract.

3. OBJECTIVES

The objectives of this policy and procedure are as follows, i.e.:

3.1 Provide for a guideline for management to deal, proactively, with instances of medical incapacity.

3.2 Identify situations of incapacity and/or inability to perform and to take actions as may be necessary in the interest of the Company, as well as the interest of the employee.

3.3 Evaluate such situation with regard to the circumstances of each particular case.

3.4 Comply with the standards of substantive and procedural fairness.

3.5 Terminate services of employment, if necessary, on a fair and rational basis.

Step 1 Investigation and Preparatory Actions

- Conduct a preliminary investigation/evaluation, as follows:

    - The ambit and extent of the medical incapacity;
    - Further medical evidence;
    - Gather information in respect of the ability to perform duties;
    - Is there full or partial compliance with common law duties?
    - Sick leave records and availability of such leave entitlement.

Step 2 Counselling the Employee

- Meet and counsel the employee in order to develop a course of action.
- Identify the medical incapacity whether it is of a temporary or permanent nature, and discuss the impairment on the employee's ability to perform duties.
- Adapt a collaborative joint problem solving technique.
- In particular communicate and traverse the guidelines above, i.e.:
    - Degree of incapacity
    - The permanence or temporary nature thereof
    - Capability of performing the work
    - Alternatives, and possible re-deployment
    - Record the meeting, outcome and plan of action in writing
    - The attached checklist is applicable in this process.

Step 3 Review Process

- Continue to council the employee and continue to consider alternatives, based on the severity of the individual incapacity, possible rehabilitation, and future compliance with contractual obligations and duties.
- Dependent on the degree of incapacity, the employee should be given a notification that continued employment could be at risk as a result of poor health and/or medical incapacity.

Step 4 Enquiry and Final Evaluation

- Should the situation not improve (or should termination of employment for reasons of medical incapacity be inevitable) arrange for a final enquiry in order to consider the position. The main function of the enquiry will be to finally assess all the circumstances and to decide whether the employee's services should be terminated, or whether feasible alternatives to termination of employment exist.

Schedule of Forms

- Form: Ill Health/Incapacity – Assessment of the Problem

ILL HEALTH/INCAPACITY - BASIC ASSESSMENT

	ILL HEALTH/INCAPACITY - BASIC ASSESSMENT	NOTES
CHECKLIST	1. Nature of incapacity and degree of severity	
	2. Likelihood of recover/period of absence	
	3. Job Title and effect on employer's operation	
	4. Sick leave entitlement	
	5. Medical incapacity or other (e.g., drug abuse)	
	6. Effect on employment/salary/career?	
	7. Cause of incapacity and estimated duration	
	8. Notes on Items 10 & 11 of the Code, i.e.: 8.1 Temporary or permanent disability? 8.2 Nature of incapacity/illness? 8.3 Recovery prognosis? 8.4 Alternatives?	 ________ ________ ________ ________
9. **ADDITIONAL NOTES:** ________________ ________________ ________________		
10. **Assessment done by** ____________		**Date** ________

SAMPLE

ALCOHOL & DRUG USAGE POLICY

1. INTRODUCTION AND APPLICATION

1.1 The employer endeavours to ensure that employees' use of either alcohol or drugs does not impair the safe and efficient running of the organization or the health and safety of its employees.

1.2 This policy applies to all employees, whether they are employed at Company premises or deployed remotely. An absolute premium is placed on mutual trust and transparency and that employees are required to communicate problems that might be experienced with regard to alcohol and drug usage, directly to management at the earliest opportunity.

1.3 The employer has a duty to provide for a safe workplace. The consumption of alcohol and drugs can result in unsafe working and injury, as well as poor productivity and efficiency. The policy seeks to ensure that it is in compliance with legislative requirements in relation to safety and health.

1.4 The aim is to prevent employees, inclusive of WFH employees, who are under the influence of drugs and alcohol from performing work, and to implement an effective process to identify and manage situations where fitness for work may be compromised by the effects of drugs or alcohol.

1.5 In particular, the employer faces challenges in respect of monitoring of possible alcohol and drug abuse where employees are performing work remotely, in accordance with WFH practice and procedure, and strict measures will be implemented in order to ensure a safe WFH environment and optimal productivity of employees.

1.6 The employer will not tolerate employees who are intoxicated whilst performing duties and should the same occur, such will constitute material breach of contract.

1.7 Dependent on the circumstances of each individual case, the employer's disciplinary code, counselling procedure or procedure for medical incapacity may be initiated.

2. INVESTIGATION, INTERVENTION AND PROBLEM SOLVING

2.1 Supervisors and managers who are of the opinion that an employee's unsatisfactory performance may be drug or alcohol related must arrange to hold a meeting with the employee. At the meeting the unsatisfactory performance or conduct and *"indicators"* of substance abuse, must be discussed. The Company's required standards as well as the breach of contract and the unacceptable situation must be emphasized. In doing so the welfare of the employee, fellow employees, safety and health and the interests of the Employer must be highlighted.

2.2 All employees regardless of seniority, are assured of absolute confidentiality and discretion in the management of reported cases of alcohol and/or drug dependence, and the employer guarantees to take the necessary remedial steps.

3. PROCEDURE

3.1 A brief history of the problem needs to be compiled on the basis of the investigation conducted.

3.2 The investigation results will indicate to management the procedure to be followed i.e. either for misconduct or for medical incapacity. Once management has made an election as to the applicable procedure and the appropriate steps to be taken, i.e. a disciplinary hearing, or counselling and/or medical assistance.

4. MEDICAL INCAPACITY: CLASSIFICATION AND TREATMENT

4.1 Should the employee admit that he/she has a substance abuse problem, this will be on the understanding that:

4.1.1 Whilst undergoing treatment, the normal sick leave entitlement will apply;

4.1.2 Every effort must be made to ensure that on completion of an applicable recovery program the employee can return to the same or equivalent work.

4.2 Should such a return jeopardize either a satisfactory level of job performance or the employee's recovery, the Company will review the circumstances surrounding the case and decide on a course of action to be taken; this may include the offer of suitable alternative employment. In exceptional circumstances, the consideration of dismissal on the grounds of ill health may be taken after alternatives have been considered and a full medical investigation has been conducted. If the employee declines to allow the Company access to relevant medical records a decision with regard to future employment will be made with the information that is available to the Company.

5. RELAPSE

5.1 Where an employee, having received treatment, suffers a relapse, the Company will consider the case on its individual merits. Medical advice will be sought in an attempt to ascertain how much more treatment/ rehabilitation time is likely to be required for a full recovery. At the

Company's discretion more treatment or rehabilitation time may be given in order to help the employee to recover fully.

6. **RECOVERY UNLIKELY**

6.1 If, after the employee have received treatment and recovery seems unlikely, the Company may wish to expedite matters for operational reasons. In such cases, termination of employment with notice may result, but in most cases a clear warning will be given to the employee beforehand and a full medical investigation will have been undertaken.

7. **MISCONDUCT AS A RESULT OF INTOXICATION**

7.1 If an employee is known to be, or strongly suspected of being intoxicated by alcohol or drug usage during working hours, management must be alerted and consulted. Arrangements will be made for the employee to be escorted from the Company premises immediately.

7.2 Disciplinary action will take place when the employee has had time to recover and to become sober, on the basis of serious and material breach of contract.

7.3 Consumption of alcohol or drug usage on the premises is illegal and a contravention of the Occupational Health and Safety Act. All employees are, under normal circumstances, expressly prohibited to consume alcohol on the premises. Any breach of this rule will result in disciplinary action being taken which is likely to result in summary dismissal.

7.4 At such times, employees will still be expected to behave in a responsible manner. Drivers are advised, where necessary, to find alternative means of transport home.

8. **DRUG ABUSE ON THE PREMISES, OR AT THE WFH OFFICE**

8.1 Employees who take drugs, which have not been prescribed on medical grounds will, in the absence of mitigating circumstances, be deemed to be committing an act of gross misconduct and will thus render themselves likely to be summarily dismissed as will any employee believed to be buying or selling drugs, or in possession of unlawful (i.e., non-prescribed) drugs. This will also constitute a statutory offence.

9. **CONCLUSION**

9.1 Employees who recognise that they have an alcohol or drug problem, or that they are at risk of developing one, must be encouraged to come forward for confidential assistance. Employees also have a contractual duty of good faith to inform the employer accordingly.

9.2 It is also recognized that WFH ("Work from Home") employees are more in a position to abuse alcohol and/or drugs and that the employer has a duty to monitor WFH employees' behaviour and work performance during working hours, at their respective homes. Such employee also has the implied contractual obligation to inform the employer of any substance abuse issue and/or problem that such employee may experience, and the failure to do so will result in breach of contract.

SAMPLE

HEALTH AND SAFETY AND MEDICAL EXAMINATION POLICY AND GUIDELINE

1. INTRODUCTION

1.1 The employer has a contractual duty in terms of the contract of employment obligations, to provide the employee with a safe and healthy work environment.

1.2 In addition the employer and employees both have statutory duties and obligations in accordance with the provisions of safety and health legislation inclusive of regulations thereto, that may be promulgated from time to time. These duties and obligations apply irrespective as to whether employees are employed at company premises, or if they work from home.

1.3 **Employees specifically have a duty to:**

1.3.1 Work safely and to protect themselves and those working with them from harm and/or potential harm.

1.3.2 Abide by and to act in accordance with statutory and/or company rules and regulations aimed at disease, or viral containment, and safety measures introduced to prevent, curb and/or to eliminate the same.

1.3.3 Comply with the reasonable requests and/or instructions of the employer issued in the furtherance of health and safety measures, either in the interest of the employee, fellow employees, management or in the public interest as the case may be.

1.4 **The employer specifically:**

1.4.1 Is committed to the welfare and health of the employees, to preventing and reducing the risk of contamination, illness, the spread of any disease or pandemic, injury on duty and the accidental loss of any of its resources and physical assets.

1.4.2 Will comply with reasonable statutory safety and health requirements as they also relate to planning, operation and maintenance of facilities and equipment.

1.4.3 Will act in the interest of society as a whole if called upon to do so, and in accordance with its own discretion, with due cognizance of legal parameters.

2. APPLICABLE LEGISLATION

2.1 The Constitution provides for the overarching right to bodily integrity and includes the right to security in, and control over one's body.

2.2 The Employment Equity Act (the "EEA") provides for a general prohibition in respect of medical testing of employees. Section 7(1) of the EEA prohibits medical testing unless legislation permits or requires such testing, or if it is "justifiable in the light of medical facts, employment conditions, social policy, the fair distribution of employee benefits or the inherent requirements of the job".

2.3 Section 7 of the EEA accordingly recognizes two exceptions to the general prohibition on medical testing:

2.3.1 Where medical testing is permitted by legislation; or

2.3.2 Where medical testing is justifiable in the light of medical facts, employment conditions, social policy, or the inherent requirements of a job. In terms of this policy the employer reserves the right to request and to demand that employees submit themselves to medical testing as a result of medical facts, employment conditions for the requirements of a certain employment position.

2.4 In terms of the provisions of this policy medical "testing" must not be confused with medical "treatment". In addition, employment legislation does not specifically regulate when an employer may require an employee to undergo medical treatment. "Medical treatment" is a different process and includes the administration of a vaccine.

2.5 The National Health Act ("NHA") provides that a health service cannot be provided to a person without consent. In terms of this policy it is acknowledged that the consent requirement is not absolute, and that the same can be overruled, if a refusal could result in a serious risk to public health or the population at large.

2.6 It is further acknowledged that section 8 of the Occupational Health and Safety Act ("OHSA"), places a general duty on employers to provide and maintain a working environment that is safe and does not pose a risk to the health of their employees. Section 8(2)(b) of the OHSA also places a duty on employers to take all reasonable steps available to eliminate or mitigate any health hazards or potential health hazards to the safety of their employees, before resorting to the use of personal protective equipment (PPR). The elimination of hazards before resorting to the use of PPE is a primary obligation placed on employers by the provisions of the OHSA.

3. MEDICAL EXAMINATIONS

3.1 This policy recognizes that the employer cannot force an employee to undergo a medical examination. However, if the Company has valid reason to demand such examination (in view of the employment and medical history of the employee) and such employee refuses to cooperate, such refusal will constitute a breach of contract and could result in the termination of employment.

3.2 The Company's policies and procedures in respect of incapacity and inability to comply with contractual obligations for reasons of ill-health will also be applicable in this regard.

4. VACCINATIONS

4.1 The obligation to ensure that the workplace is a safe and healthy environment conducive to optimal productivity rests primarily with the employer. Decisions in respect of mandatory vaccinations, medical testing and medical treatment can and will be made dependent on prevailing circumstances and applicable legislation.

4.2 The OHSA requires an employer to provide and to maintain a safe and healthy work environment both for the employees as well as for other persons who have access to its premises, such as clients, suppliers or contractors. On this basis the Company can refuse entry to the premises of any person who may have positive symptoms in respect of any health threat, and/or provide for access measures to the premises in this respect.

4.3 With regard to voluntary vaccinations, the Company reserves the right to require from employees (on a consensual basis) to provide documentary proof of the date and administering of such vaccination (if the same was in fact administered). The employee's vaccination status would constitute health information in terms of the Protection of Personal Health Act ("POPI") and can only be processed by the employer in limited instances, with the consent of an employee. Such consent shall not unreasonably be withheld by the employee.

4.4 In respect of mandatory vaccinations, consultations will take place individually or collectively with employees in order to reach agreement with due regard to all circumstances, inclusive of the public interest and public health considerations, as well as statutory regulations and measures.

5. CONCLUSION

5.1 Safety and health issues will, as far as practicably possible, be dealt with on a collaborative, consultative and consensual basis, either individually or collectively.

5.2 Employees will be consulted should it become necessary for vaccines to be administered and for medical testing to be conducted as provided for in law. The Company reserves the right to introduce the necessary health and safety measures in compliance with statutory directives and protocols as the case may be.

5.3 Where it becomes necessary for a medical examination to be conducted in order to establish the employment capacity and status of the employee, and in order to obtain medical evidence for the purposes of deciding on continued employment, the employee's consent will still be required, but in the absence of such consent the Company reserves the right to make a decision on the employee's future employment, without the requested medical records.

5.4 The employer's general obligations in respect of health and safety, inclusive of those stated in this policy, will be complied with in the context of the employee's rights to freedom of conscience, religion and beliefs. Such rights and beliefs will be practically and reasonably accommodated, in the interests of the employee, the employer and the public interest, as the case may be, and with due regard to all prevailing circumstances.

Statutory Regulations

BCEA1A

(Regulation 2)

BASIC CONDITIONS OF EMPLOYMENT ACT, 1997 SUMMARY TO BE KEPT BY AN EMPLOYER IN TERMS OF SECTION 30

The following is a summary of the provisions of the most important sections of the Basic Conditions of Employment Act, 1997, as amended.

1. APPLICATION OF THE ACT: SECTION 3

The Act applies to all employees and employers except members of the State Security Agency and unpaid volunteers working for an organisation with a charitable purpose.

The basic conditions of employment contained in the Act form part of the contract of employment of employees covered by the Act. Some, but not all, basic conditions of employment may be varied by individual or collective agreements in accordance with the provisions of the Act. (See paragraph 7 below).

2. REGULATION OF WORKING TIME: CHAPTER TWO

2.1 Application

This chapter does not apply to senior managerial employees, employees engaged as sales staff who travel and employees who work less than 24 hours a month.

2.2 Ordinary hours of work: Section 9 and 9A

2.2.1 No employer shall require or permit an employee to work more than- a) 45 hours in any week;

b) nine hours in any day if an employee works for five days or less in a week; or

c) eight hours in any day if an employee works on more than five days in a week.

2.2.2 Employees earning less than the threshold, who works for less than four hours on any day must be paid for four hours on that day

2.3 **Overtime: Section 10**

2.3.1 An employer may not require or permit an employee

(a) to work overtime except by an agreement;

(b) to work more than ten hours' overtime a week.

2.3.2 An agreement may not require or permit an employee to work more than 12 hours on any day.

2.3.3 A collective agreement may increase overtime to fifteen hours per week for up to two months in any period of 12 months.

2.3.4 Overtime must be paid at 1.5 times the employee's normal wage or an employee may agree to receive paid time off.

2.4 Compressed working **week**: Section **11**

2.4.1 An employee may agree in writing to work up to 12 hours in a day without receiving overtime pay.

2.4.2 This agreement may not require or permit an employee to work-

(a) more than 45 ordinary hours in any week;

(b) more than ten hours' overtime in any week; or

(c) more than five days in any week.

2.5 **Averaging of hours of work: Section 12**

2.5.1 A collective agreement may permit the hours of work to be averaged over a period of up to four months.

2.5.2 An employee who is bound by **such** a collective agreement may not work more than

(a) an average of 45 ordinary hours in a week over the agreed period;

(b) an average of five hours' overtime in a week over the agreed period.

2.6 **Meal intervals: Section 14**

2.6.1 An employee must have a meal interval of 60 minutes after five hours work.

2.6.2 A written agreement may-

(a) reduce the meal interval to 30 minutes;

(b) dispense with the meal interval for employees who work fewer than six hours on a day.

2.7 **Daily and weekly rest period: Section 15**

An employee must have a daily rest period of 12 consecutive hours and a weekly rest period of 36 consecutive hours, which, unless otherwise agreed, must include Sunday.

2.8 **Pay for work on Sundays: Section 16**

2.8.1 An employee who occasionally works on a Sunday must receive double pay.

2.8.2 An employee who ordinarily works on a Sunday must be paid at 1.5 times the normal wage.

2.8.3 Paid time off in return for working on a Sunday may be agreed upon.

2.9 **Night work: Section 17**

2.9.1 Employees who work at night between 18h00 and 06h00 must be compensated by payment of an allowance or by a reduction of working hours and transport must be available.

2.9.2 Employees who work regularly after 23:00 and before 06:00 the next day must be informed-

(a) of any health and safety hazards; and

(b) the right to undergo a medical examination.

2.10 **Public holidays: Section 18**

2.10.1 Employees must be paid their ordinary pay for any public holiday that falls on a working day.

2.10.2 Work on a public holiday is by agreement and paid at double the rate.

2.10.3 A public holiday may be exchanged with another day by agreement.

3. LEAVE: CHAPTER THREE

3.1 **Application**

The chapter on leave does not apply to an employee who works less than 24 hours a month for an employer and to leave granted in excess of the leave entitlement under this chapter.

3.2 **Annual leave: Sections 20 & 21**

3.2.1 Employees are entitled to 21 consecutive days' annual leave or by agreement, one day for every 17 days worked or one hour for every 17 hours worked.

3.2.2 Leave must be granted not later than six months after the end of the annual leave cycle.

3.2.3 An employer must not pay an employee instead of granting leave except on termination of employment.

3.3 **Sick leave: Sections 22 - 24**

3.3.1 An employee is entitled to six weeks' paid sick leave in a period of 36 months.

3.3.2 During the first six months an employee is entitled to one day's paid sick leave for every 26 days worked.

3.3.3 An employer may require a medical certificate before paying an employee who is absent for more than two consecutive days or who is frequently absent.

3.4 **Maternity leave: Sections 25 & 26**

3.4.1 A pregnant employee is entitled to four consecutive months' maternity leave.

3.4.2 A pregnant employee or employee nursing her child is not allowed to perform work that is hazardous to her or her child.

3.5 **Parental Leave: Section 25A**

3.5.1 An employee, who is a parent of a child, is entitled to at least ten consecutive days parental leave, when the employee's child is born, or adoption is granted; or the child is placed in the care of a prospective adoptive parent by a competent court, pending the finalization of an adoption order.

3.6 **Adoption Leave: Section 25B**

3.6.1 An employee who is an adoptive parent of a child who is below the age of two, is subject to section 25(6), entitled to at least ten weeks consecutive adoptive leave; or ten consecutive days parental leave when adoptive is granted, or the child is placed in his/her care as prospective adoptive parent by a competent court, pending the finalization of an adoptive order.

3.7 **Commissioning parental Leave: Section 25C**

3.7.1 An employee, who is a commissioning parent in a surrogate motherhood agreement is subject to section 25(6), entitled to at least ten weeks consecutive commissioning parental leave; or ten consecutive days parental leave when his/her child is born as a result of a surrogate motherhood agreement

3.8 **Family responsibility leave: Section 27**

3.8.1 Full time employees are entitled to three days paid family responsibility leave per year, on request, when the employee's child is born or sick, or in the event of the death of the employee's spouse or life partner, or the employee's parent, adoptive parent, grandparent, child, adopted child, grandchild or sibling.

3.8.2 **An employer may require reasonable proof.**

4. PARTICULARS OF EMPLOYMENT AND REMUNERATION: CHAPTER FOUR

4.1 Application

This chapter does not apply to an employee who works less than 24 hours a month for an employer.

4.2 **Written particulars of employment: Section 29**

4.2.1 An employer must supply an employee when the employee commences employment, with the following particulars in writing:

(a) full name and address of the employer;
(b) name and occupation of the employee, or a brief description of the work;
(c) various places of work;
(d) date of employment;
(e) ordinary hours of work and days of work;
(f) wage or the rate and method of calculating;
(g) rate for overtime work;
(h) any other cash payments;
(i) any payment in kind and the value thereof;
(j) frequency of remuneration;
(k) Any deductions;
(l) leave entitlement;
(m) period of notice or period of contract;
(n) description of any council or sectoral determination which covers the employer's business:
(o) period of employment with a previous employer that counts towards the period of employment;
(p) list of any other documents that form part of the contract, indicating a place where a copy of each may be obtained.

4.2.2 Particulars must be revised if the terms of employment change.

4.3 **Informing employees of their rights: Section 30**

A statement of employees' rights must be displayed at the workplace in official languages used at the workplace.

4.4 **Keeping of records: Section 31**

Every employer must keep a record containing the following information:

(a) employee's name and occupation;
(b) time worked;
(c) remuneration paid;
(d) date of birth if under 18 years of age; and
(e) any other prescribed information.

4.5 **Information about remuneration: Section 33**

The following information must be given in writing when the employee is paid:

(a) employer's name and address;
(b) employee's name and occupation;
(c) period of payment;

(d) remuneration in money;
(e) any deduction made from the remuneration;
(f) the actual amount paid; and
(g) if relevant to the calculation of that employee's remuneration-
   (i) employee's rate of remuneration and overtime rate;
   (ii) number of ordinary and overtime hours worked during the period of payment;
   (iii) number of hours worked on a Sunday or public holiday during that period; and
   (iv) if an agreement to average working time has been concluded, the total number of ordinary and overtime hours worked in the period of averaging.

4.6 **Deductions and other acts concerning remuneration: Sections 34 and 34A**

4.6.1 An employer may not deduct money from an employee's remuneration unless -
   (a) The employee agrees in writing to the deduction of a specific debt;
   (b) The deduction is made in terms of a collective agreement, law, court order or arbitration award

4.6.2 A deduction in respect of damage or loss caused by the employee may only be made with agreement and after the employer has followed a fair procedure

4.6.3 Employers must pay deductions and employer contributions to benefit funds to the fund within seven days.

4.7 **Calculation of remuneration and wages: Section 35**

4.7.1 Wages are calculated by the number of hours ordinarily worked.

4.7.2 Monthly remuneration or wage is four and one-third times the weekly wage.

4.7.3 If calculated on a basis other than time, or if the employee's remuneration or wage fluctuates significantly from period to period, any payment must be calculated by reference to remuneration or wage during-
   (a) the preceding 13 weeks; or
   (b) if employed for a shorter period, that period.

4.7.4 Employers and employees should consult a schedule published in the Government Gazette to determine whether a particular category of payment forms part of an employee's remuneration for the purpose of calculations made in terms of this Act.

5. TERMINATION OF EMPLOYMENT: CHAPTER FIVE

5.1 Application

This chapter does not apply to an employee who works less than 24 hours in a month for an employer.

5.2 Notice of termination of employment: Section 37

5.2.1 A contract of employment may be terminated on notice of not less than-

(a) one week, if the employee has been employed for six months or less;

(b) two weeks, if the employee has been employed for more than six months but not more than one year;

(c) four weeks, if the employee has been employed for one year or more, or if a farm worker or domestic worker has been employed for more than six months.

5.2.2 A collective agreement may shorten the four weeks' notice period to not less than two weeks.

5.2.3 Notice must be given in writing except when it is given by an illiterate employee.

5.2.4 The notice on termination of employment by an employer in terms of the Act does not prevent the employee challenging the fairness or lawfulness of the dismissal in terms of the Labour Relations Act, 1995 or any other law.

5.3 Severance pay: Section 41

An employee dismissed for operational requirements or whose contract of employment is terminated in terms of section 38 of the Insolvency Act, 1936 is entitled to one week's severance pay for every year of service.

5.4 Certificate of Service: Section 42

On termination of employment an employee is entitled to a certificate of service.

6. PROHIBITION OF EMPLOYMENT OF CHILDREN AND FORCED LABOUR SECTIONS 43 - 48

6.1 It is a criminal offence to employ a child under 15 years of age.

6.2 Children under 18 may not be employed to do work inappropriate for their age or that places them at risk.

6.3 Causing, demanding or requiring forced labour is a criminal offence.

7. VARIATION OF BASIC CONDITIONS OF EMPLOYMENT: SECTIONS 49- 50

7.1 A collective agreement concluded by a bargaining council may replace or exclude any basic condition of employment except the following:
   - (a) the duty to arrange working time with regard to the health and safety and family responsibility of employees (S.7,9 and 13);
   - (b) reduce the protection afforded to employees who perform night work (S. 17(3) and (4));
   - (c) reduce annual leave to less than two weeks (S. 20);
   - (d) reduce entitlement to maternity leave (S 25};
   - (e) reduce entitlement to sick leave to the extent permitted (S. 22-24); and
   - (f) prohibition of child and forced labour (S.48).

7.2 Collective agreements and individual agreements may only replace or exclude basic conditions of employment to the extent permitted by the Act or a sectoral determination (S.49).

7.3 The Minister of Labour may make a determination to vary or exclude a basic condition of employment. This can also be done on application by an employer or employer organisation (S. 50).

7.4 A determination may not be granted unless a trade union representing the employees has consented to the variation or has had the opportunity to make representations to the Minister. A copy of any determination must be displayed by the employer at the work place and must be made available to employee's (S.50).

8. SECTORAL DETERMINATIONS: SECTION 51

Sectoral determinations may be made to establish basic conditions for employees in a sector and area.

9. MONITORING, ENFORCEMENT AND LEGAL PROCEEDINGS: SECTIONS 63 - 81

9.1 Labour inspectors must advise employees and employers on their rights and obligations in terms of employment laws. They conduct inspections, investigate complaints and may question persons and inspect, copy and remove records and other relevant documents (S. 64 - 66).

9.2 An inspector may serve a compliance order on an employer who is not complying with a provision of the Act, the National Minimum Wage Act, 2018, the Unemployment Insurance Act or the Unemployment Insurance Contributions Act. The order may be made an Arbitration Award. (S. 68 - 73).

9.3 Employees may not be discriminated against for exercising their rights in terns of the Act (S. 78 - 81).

10. PRESUMPTION AS TO WHO IS AN EMPLOYEE: SECTION 83A

10.1 A person who works for, or provides services to, another person is presumed to be an employee if -

(a) his or her manner or hours of work are subject to control or direction;

(b) he or she forms part of the employer's organisation;

(c) he or she has worked for the other person for at least 40 hours per month over the previous three months;

(d) he or she is economically dependant on the other person;

(e) he or she is provided with his or her tools or work equipment; or

(f) he or she only works for, or renders service to, one person.

10.1 If one of these factors is present, the person is presumed to be an employee until the employer proves that he or she is not.

11. GENERAL

It is an offence to-

(a) obstruct or attempt to influence improperly a person who is performing a function in terms of the Act:

(b) obtain or attempt to obtain any prescribed document by means of fraud, false pretences, or by presenting or submitting a false or forged document;

(c) pretend to be a labour inspector or any other person performing a function in terms of the Act;

(d) refuse or fail to answer fully any lawful question put by a labour inspector or any other person performing a function in terms of the Act;

(e) hinder or obstruct a labour inspector or any other person performing a function in terms of the Act. (S. 92}

SCHEDULE 8 OF LABOUR RELATIONS ACT

CODE OF GOOD PRACTICE: DISMISSAL

[Schedule 8 amended bys. 57 of Act No. 42 of 1996 and bys. 56 of Act No. 12 of 2002.]

1. Introduction

(1) This code of good practice deals with some of the key aspects of dismissal for reasons related to conduct and capacity. It is intentionally general. Each case is unique, and departures from the norms established by this Code may be justified in proper circumstances. For example, the number of employees employed in an establishment may warrant a different approach.

(2) This Act emphasises the primary of collective agreements. This Code is not intended as a substitute for disciplinary codes and procedures where these are the subject of collective agreements, or the outcome of joint decision-making by an employer and a work-place forum.

(3) The key principle in this Code is that employers and employees should treat one another with mutual respect. A premium is placed on both employment justice and the efficient operation of business. While employees should be protected from arbitrary action, employers are entitled to satisfactory conduct and work performance from their employees.

2. Fair reasons for dismissal

(1) A dismissal is unfair if it is not effected for a fair reason and in accordance with a fair procedure, even if it complies with any notice period in a contract of employment or in legislation governing employment. Whether or not a dismissal is for a fair reason is determined by the facts of the case, and the appropriateness of dismissal as a penalty. Whether or not the procedure is fair is determined by referring to the guidelines set out below.

(2) This Act recognises three grounds on which a termination of employment might be legitimate. These are: the conduct of the employee, the capacity of the employee, and the operational requirements of the employer's business.

(3) This Act provides that a dismissal is automatically unfair if the reason for the dismissal is one that amounts to an infringement of the fundamental rights of employees and trade unions, or if the reason is one of those listed in section 187. The reasons include participation in a lawful strike, intended or actual pregnancy and acts of discrimination.

(4) In cases where the dismissal is not automatically unfair, the employer must show that the reason for dismissal is a reason related to the employee 's conduct or capacity, or is based on the operational requirements of the business. If the employer fails to do that, or fails to prove that the dismissal was effected in accordance with a fair procedure, the dismissal is unfair.

Disciplinary procedures prior to dismissal

3. **Disciplinary measures short of dismissal**

(1) All employers should adopt disciplinary rules that establish the standard of conduct required of their employees. The form and content of disciplinary rules will obviously vary according to the size and nature of the employer's business. In general, a larger business will require a more formal approach to discipline. An employer 's rules must create certainty and consistency in the application of discipline. This requires that the standards of conduct are clear and made available to employees in a manner that is easily understood. Some rules or standards may be so well established and known that it is not necessary to communicate them.

(2) The courts have endorsed the concept of corrective or progressive discipline. This approach regards the purpose of discipline as a means for employees to know and understand what standards are required of them. Efforts should be made to correct employees ' behaviour through a system of graduated disciplinary measures such as counselling and warnings.

(3) Formal procedures do not have to be invoked every time a rule is broken or a standard is not met. Informal advice and correction is the best and most effective way for an employer to deal with minor violations of work discipline. Repeated misconduct will warrant warnings, which themselves may be graded according to degrees of severity. More serious infringements or repeated misconduct may call for a final warning, or other action short of dismissal. Dismissal should be reserved for cases of serious misconduct or repeated offences.

4. **Dismissals for misconduct**

(4) Generally, it is not appropriate to dismiss an employee for a first offence, except if the misconduct is serious and of such gravity that it makes a continued employment relationship intolerable. Examples of serious misconduct, subject to the rule that each case should be judged on its merits, are gross dishonesty or wilful damage to the

property of the employer, wilful endangering of the safety of others physical assault on the employer, a fellow employee, client or customer and gross insubordination. Whatever the merits of the case for dismissal might be, a dismissal will not be fair if it does not meet the requirements of section 188.

(5) When deciding whether or not to impose the penalty of dismissal, the employer should in addition to the gravity of the misconduct consider factors such as the employee's circumstances (including length of service, previous disciplinary record and personal circumstances), the nature of the job and the circumstances of the infringement itself.

(6) The employer should apply the penalty of dismissal consistently with the way in which it has been applied to the same and other employees in the past, and consistently as between two or more employees who participate in the misconduct under consideration.

5. **Fair procedure**

(1) Normally, the employer should conduct an investigation to determine whether there are grounds for dismissal. This does not need to be a formal enquiry. The employer should notify the employee of the allegations using a form and language that the employee can reasonably understand. The employee should be allowed the opportunity to state a case in response to the allegations. The employee should be entitled to a reasonable time to prepare the response and to the assistance of a trade union representative or fellow employee. After the enquiry, the employer should communicate the decision taken, and preferably furnish the employee with written notification of that decision.

(2) Discipline against a trade union representative or an employee who is an office-bearer or official of a trade union should not be instituted without first informing and consulting the trade union.

(3) If the employee is dismissed, the employee should be given the reason for dismissal and reminded of any rights to refer the matter to a council with jurisdiction or to the Commission or to any dispute resolution procedures established in terms of a collective agreement.

(4) In exceptional circumstances, if the employer cannot reasonably be expected to comply with these guidelines, the employer may dispense with pre-dismissal procedures.

6. **Disciplinary records**

Employers should keep records for each employee specifying the nature of any disciplinary transgressions , the actions taken by the employer and the reasons for the actions.

7. **Dismissals and industrial action**

(1) Participation in a strike that does not comply with the provisions of chapter IV is misconduct. However, like any other act of misconduct, it does not always deserve dismissal. The substantive fairness of dismissal in these circumstances must be determined in the light of the facts of the case, including-

(a) the seriousness of the contravention of this Act ;

(b) attempts made to comply with this Act; and

(c) whether or not the strike was in response to unjustified conduct by the employer.

(2) Prior to dismissal the employer should, at the earliest opportunity, contact a trade union official to discuss the course of action it intends to adopt. The employer should issue an ultimatum in clear and unambiguous terms that should state what is required of the employees and what sanction will be imposed if they do not comply with the ultimatum . The employees should be allowed sufficient time to reflect on the ultimatum and respond to it, either by complying with it or rejecting it. If the employer cannot reasonably be expected to extend these steps to the employees in question, the employer may dispense with them.

8. **Guidelines in cases of dismissal for misconduct**

Any person who is determining whether a dismissal for misconduct is unfair should consider-

(a) whether or not the employee contravened a rule or standard regulating conduct in, or of relevance to, the work-place; and

(b) if a rule or standard was contravened, whether or not-

(i) the rule was a valid or reasonable rule or standard;

(ii) the employee was aware, or could reasonably be expected to have been aware, of the rule or standard;

(iii) the rule or standard has been consistently applied by the employer; and

(iv) dismissal with an appropriate sanction for the contravention of the rule or standard.

9. **Probation**

(1) (a) An employer may require a newly-hired employee to serve a period of probation before the appointment of the employee is confirmed.

(b) The purpose of probation is to give the employer an opportunity to evaluate the employee's performance before confirming the appointment.

(c) Probation should not be used for purposes not contemplated by this Code to deprive employees of the status of permanent employment. For example, a practice of dismissing employees who complete their probation periods and replacing them with newly-hired employees, is not consistent with the purpose of probation and constitutes an unfair labour practice.

(d) The period of probation should be determined in advance and be of reasonable duration. The length of the probationary period should be determined with reference to the nature of the job and the time it takes to determine the employee's suitability for continued employment.

(e) During the probationary period, the employee's performance should be assessed. An employer should give an employee reasonable evaluation, instruction, training, guidance or counselling in order to allow the employee to render a satisfactory service.

(f) If the employer determines that the employee's performance is below standard, the employer should advise the employee of any aspects in which the employer considers the employee to be failing to meet the required performance standards. If the employer believes that the employee is incompetent, the employer should advise the employee of the respects in which the employee is not competent. The employer may either extend the probationary period or dismiss the employee after complying with subitems (g) or (h), as the case may be.

(g) The period of probation may only be extended for a reason that relates to the purpose of probation. The period of extension should not be disproportionate to the legitimate purpose that the employer seeks to achieve.

(h) An employer may only decide to dismiss an employee or extend the probationary period after the employer has invited the employee to make representations and has considered any representations made. A trade union representative or fellow employee may make the representations on behalf of the employee.

(i) If the employer decides to dismiss the employee or to extend the probationary period, the employer should advise the employee of his or her rights to refer the matter to a council having jurisdiction, or to the Commission.

(j) Any person making a decision about the fairness of a dismissal of an employee for poor work performance during or on expiry of the probationary period ought to accept reasons for dismissal that may be less compelling than would be the case in dismissals effected after the completion of the probationary period.

(2) After probation, an employee should not be dismissed for unsatisfactory performance unless the employer has-

(a) given the employee appropriate evaluation, instruction, training, guidance or counselling; and
(b) after a reasonable period of time for improvement, the employee continues to perform unsatisfactorily.
(3) The procedure leading to dismissal should include an investigation to establish the reasons for the unsatisfactory performance and the employer should consider other ways, short of dismissal, to remedy the matter.
(4) In the process, the employee should have the right to be heard and to be assisted by a trade union representative or a fellow employee.

10. **Guidelines in cases of dismissal for poor work performance.-**

Any person determining whether a dismissal for poor work performance is unfair should consider-
(a) whether or not the employee failed to meet a performance standard; and
(b) if the employee did not meet a required performance standard whether or not-
   (i) the employee was aware, or could reasonably be expected to have been aware, of the required performance standard;
   (ii) the employee was given a fair opportunity to meet the required performance standard; and
   (iii) dismissal was an appropriate sanction for not meeting the required performance standard.

11. **Incapacity: Ill health and injury.-**

(1) Incapacity on the grounds of ill health or injury may be temporary or permanent. If an employee is temporarily unable to work in these circumstances, the employer should investigate the extent of the incapacity or the injury. If the employee is likely to be absent for a time that is unreasonably long in the circumstances, the employer should investigate all the possible alternatives short of dismissal. When alternatives are considered, relevant factors might include the nature of the job, the period of absence, the seriousness of the illness or injury and the possibility of securing a temporary replacement for the ill or injured employee. In cases of permanent incapacity, the employer should ascertain the possibility of securing alternative

employment, or adapting the duties or work circumstances of the employee to accommodate the employee 's disability.

(2) In the process of the investigation referred to in subsection (1) the employee should be allowed the opportunity to state a case in response and to be assisted by a trade union representative or fellow employee.

(3) The degree of incapacity is relevant to the fairness of any dismissal. The cause of the incapacity may also be relevant. In the case of certain kinds of incapacity, for example alcoholism or drug abuse, counselling and rehabilitation may be appropriate steps for an employer to consider.

(4) Particular consideration should be given to employees who are injured at work or who are incapacitated by work-related illness. The courts have indicated that the duty on the employer to accommodate the incapacity of the employee is more onerous in these circumstances.

12. **Guidelines in cases of dismissal arising from ill health or injury.**

Any person determining whether a dismissal arising from ill health or injury is unfair should consider-

(a) whether or not the employee is capable of performing the work; and

(b) if the employee is not capable-

(i) the extent to which the employee is able to perform the work;

(ii) the extent to which the employee 's work circumstances might be adapted to accommodate disability, or, where this is not possible, the extent to which the employee 's duties might be adapted; and

(iii) the availability of any suitable alternative work.

BIBLIOGRAPHY

Aikin, O. (1992). *Contracts.* Exeter: Short Run Press Ltd.

ANON. (2011). *Practical Guide to Human Resource Management.* Johannesburg: Fleet Street Publications.

Du Toit, D., Fredman, S., Bhatia, G., Cherupara-Vaddekkethil, A., & Osiki, A. (2020). *Fairwork Project: Code of Good Practice for the Regulation of Platform Work in South Africa.* Available online: https://fair.work/wp-content/uploads/sites/97/2020/11/South-Africa_Code-of-Good-Practice_Full.pdf

Du Toit, D., Godfrey, S. Cooper, C., Giles, G., Cohen, T., Conradie, B. & Steenkamp, A. (2014). *Labour Relations Law: A Comprehensive Guide* (6th ed.). Durban: Lexis Nexis.

Fouche, M. (2015). *Rules of the CCMA and the Labour Courts* (4th ed.). Durban: Lexis Nexis

GilesFiles. (2020). *GilesFiles Law Reports.* Available online: https://www.gilesfiles.co.za/

Government Gazette. (2006). *Code of Good Practice: Who is an employee?* NOTICE 1774 OF 2006. Available online: https://www.labourguide.co.za/download-top/260-code-who-is-employeepdf/file

Grogan, J. (2007). *Workplace Law* (9th ed.). Claremont, Cape Town: Juta & Company Ltd.

Grogan, J. (2011). *Dismissal* (2nd impression). Claremont, Cape Town: Juta & Company Ltd.

Grogan, J. (2014). *Labour Litigation and Dispute Resolution* (2nd ed.). Claremont, Cape Town: Juta & Company Ltd.

Hofmeyr, C.D. (2020/21). *Labour Law Information Updates 2020/21.* Available online: https://www.cliffedekkerhofmeyr.com

International Labour Office. (1984). *Payment by Results.* Geneva: Publications Branch, ILO.

Le Rouxm R. (2009). *The World of Work: Forms of Engagement in South Africa.* Available online: http://www.ilera-directory.org/15thworldcongress/files/papers/Track_5/Thur_W4_LE%20ROUX.pdf

The South African Labour Guide. (2013). *Code of Good Practice: Dismissal. Schedule 8 to the Labour Relations Act 66 of 1995* (as amended). Available online: https://www.labourguide.co.za/download-top/261-code-of-good-practice-dismissalpdf/file

Van Niekerk, A. (2008). *Law @ Work.* Durban: Lexis Nexis.

Wikipedia. (n.d.). Fourth Industrial Revolution. Available online: https://en.wikipedia.org/wiki/Fourth_Industrial_Revolution

INDEX

Personally Identifiable Information (PII), 160

S

T

U

V

W

Z

www.ingramcontent.com/pod-product-compliance
Lightning Source LLC
LaVergne TN
LVHW061221100826
845148LV00004B/822

* 9 7 8 1 8 6 9 2 2 8 9 9 6 *